GARLAND STUDIES ON INDUSTRIAL PRODUCTIVITY

edited by
STUART BRUCHEY
UNIVERSITY OF MAINE

A GARLAND SERIES

LABOR UNION ELECTIONS AND CORPORATE FINANCIAL PERFORMANCE

JOHN W. MOORE

GARLAND PUBLISHING, Inc.
New York & London / 1995

Library of Congress Cataloging-in-Publication Data

Moore, John W., 1948–
    Labor union elections and corporate financial performance / John
W. Moore.
        p.   cm. — (Garland studies on industrial productivity)
    Includes bibliographical references and index.
    ISBN 0-8153-1973-8
    1. Corporations—United States—Finance.   2. Financial statements—
United States.   3. Trade-unions—United States—Recognition—Elec-
tions.   4. Disclosure in accounting—United States.   I. Title.
II. Series.
    HG4061.M66   1995
    331.87'4—dc20   94-45049
    JK   CIP

Printed on acid-free, 250-year-life paper
Manufactured in the United States of America

To Anne, Chandler, Scott, and Elisabeth, and to my parents, Merville and Helen Moore.

Contents

Preface

This book is a result of growing up in Michigan, where labor unions are found in many industrial organizations. Curiosity became research interest when life presented the opportunity to pursue a doctoral degree in the field of accounting. My dissertation research was based on the premise that accounting disclosure requirements for companies' financial statements are not perfect yet and are still evolving. Labor unions are an example of an economic force which impacts some organizations, but not others. Since the final choice of whether a company is unionized is determined by the employees, unionism differs among firms.

This leads us to question whether unionism is related to differences in companies' financial performance. If so, are the differences sufficient to require disclosure of the union linkage in the annual financial reports?

The purpose of this book is to present and discuss relationships between labor union organizations, companies which have had labor union elections, and existing accounting requirements for disclosure of information about unionism in a given company. Previous research into financial statement users' need for increased disclosure indicated that investors and analysts placed value on certain data which may be affected by unionism. Another body of research into "union effects" provided a basis for selecting certain accounting variables which may have been influenced by labor unions. These variables included profitability, research and development spending, productivity, stock prices, and compensation.

This book reports the results of tests for differences between companies with union elections compared to companies without union elections for variables from the union effects and disclosure literature. The test results support the previous calls for increased disclosure.

This work began as dissertation research, published in 1992. Subsequent research has been included to provide further insights into the link between union elections and corporate financial performance.

John W. Moore

Acknowledgments

I wish to acknowledge the generous permission of the American Accounting Association for permission to reproduce the figures and tables used in Chapter II to discuss disclosure research, and Standard and Poor's Compustat Services Inc. for permission to quote data definitions and related technical matter. The National Labor Relations Board provided the election data file, without which this research would not have been possible. I want to thank Stuart Bruchey, the editor of the Industrial Productivity Series, for his interest in this research; Robert McKenzie, my editor at Garland, for his assistance and suggestions, and Kathy Vest for word processing, patience, and good humor.

Tables

Figures

Exhibits

Labor Union
Elections and
Corporate Financial
Performance

I

Introduction

Labor unions have been a part of the American business environment for two centuries. One of the chief functions of a union is to serve as the bargaining agent for its members in contract negotiations with an employer. One purpose of such bargaining is to increase the total compensation of union members. Consequently, collective bargaining agreements can be expected to result in higher employer costs for wages, medical coverage, and retirement benefits compared to similar costs in nonunion firms (Freeman 1981). In spite of this, researchers have only recently tested unionization in companies as a possible determinant of profitability (Clark 1984, Salinger 1984, Karier 1985, Connolly, Hirsch, and Hershey 1986, Voos and Mishel 1986a, 1986b, and Becker and Olson 1992).

STATEMENT OF THE PROBLEM

This study addressed disclosure of company-specific data regarding individual firm contracts with labor unions within the annual financial statements. Prior research on disclosure has provided several data items which various users of financial statements have indicated they wished to see disclosed in a firm's financial statements. Those studies indicated that equity investors and security analysts placed value on certain data which may be affected by organized labor, including research expenditures and information on labor contracts (Singhvi and Desai 1971), and pension plans and research and development expenditures (Buzby 1974). However, publicly held companies in the United States are not currently required to disclose such data in their financial statements.

A body of research on "union effects" provided a basis for selection of certain variables which may have been influenced by labor unions. Those studies have indicated the existence of a "union effect," and provided evidence that having one's employees belong to a union

3

may have resulted in changes in a number of measures of financial performance compared to nonunion firms. These measures include profitability (Clark 1984, Salinger 1984, Karier 1985, Becker and Olson 1992); expenditures for research and development (Connolly, Hirsch, and Hirschey 1986, Allen 1988, Hirsch 1992); productivity (Brown and Medoff 1978, Clark 1980, Clark 1984, Hirsch and Link 1984, Mitchell and Stone 1992), stock prices (Ruback and Zimmerman 1984, Bronars and Deere 1990, Hirsch and Morgan 1994); and compensation (Freeman 1981, Belman and Voos 1993).

This study tested for differences between firms with union elections compared to firms without union elections for variables from the union effects and disclosure literature. The data were for the period of 1978-1987. The variables tested were research and development spending per employee, pension and retirement expenditures per employee, return on investment, and sales per employee. Data definitions are given in Appendix A. Two of the variables, sales and return on investment, are influenced by many factors other than labor union activity. Sales is influenced by product type and market, general condition of the economy, competition, and credit availability, to name a few. Return on investment is a function of both investment in assets and net income. Net income in turn is influenced by factors beyond the control of management. The other two variables, research and development spending and pension and retirement expenditures, are more directly controllable by management, but may be influenced by the union (particularly pensions, because this is a negotiable item during contract bargaining). Research and development spending and pension and retirement expenditures share a relationship in that both are internally determined. Earlier research on union effects (Connolly, Hirsch and Hirschey, 1986) found that R&D spending was influenced by unionism. A separate study, with a different population, found that pensions, as a component of compensation, were influenced by the presence of a labor union (Freeman and Medoff, 1981). No research has been found which tested these variables together on the same population for a widely defined population.

Combining the lack of disclosure about unions with the evidence of union effects, the research question in this study was whether representation or decertification labor elections have an impact on the financial statements. The results of the test should either support or refute the prior calls for disclosure (Singhvi and Desai 1971; Buzby

1974). Evidence that these union elections are associated with measurable changes in financial performance (in either direction) would support the idea that there are accounting disclosure needs which are not currently served. That in turn would suggest the possibility that information about union elections should be disclosed in a uniform and consistent manner in the financial statements.

Therefore, the first step in empirical testing was a univariate pretest-posttest of financial results before and after a union election for a group of publicly traded firms. The initial vote on whether to be represented by a labor union is called a representation election. Subsequently, employees may vote to decertify the union, which is the end of the relationship. The group of firms with elections was partitioned for additional testing into subgroups with representation elections (for unions winning and for unions losing the elections) and decertification elections (for unions winning and for unions losing). The purpose of this was to determine if these "union effects" reverse or partly mitigate in those companies which, having been previously unionized, later have employees vote not to be represented any longer by their union. This study tested companies which had union elections against similar companies which had not had elections on four variables: research and development spending, pension and retirement expenditures, return on investment, and sales. In order to assure comparability, companies with union elections were compared to a control group of companies which had not had a labor election during the test period. Each firm with an election was compared to its own unique control group of companies with the same standard industrial classification (SIC) code, which shared the same fiscal year, for the same periods of data. Chapter III details the testing procedures.

ACCOUNTING PROVINCE

For information to be included in the financial statements it ought to be within the accounting domain. A great deal of information is generated at the firm level, and some of it does not apply to accounting in the sense that it is not appropriate for inclusion within the financial statements. For example, data regarding customers' names, supplier pricing, or employees' names and compensation should not be disclosed. However, what does fit within accounting's domain is fairly broad and still evolving. New accounting standards, such as for disclosure, usually contain some degree of compromise. Bernstein observed that compromise is the nature of standard-setting: "...social sciences, such as accounting is, do not have codified conceptual frameworks. There are none for law, economics, or finance. The limited areas which have been addressed so far have required a great many compromises and adjustments to contemporary conditions and forces" (1989, 54).

To help provide some remedy for this lack of a framework, the Financial Accounting Standards Board (FASB) undertook the Conceptual Framework project in the mid-1970s. The purpose of the project was to establish "...a coherent system of interrelated objectives and concepts that are expected to lead to consistent financial accounting and reporting. These concepts are expected to guide the selection of events to be accounted for, the measurement of those events as well as the means of their summarization and communication to interested users" (Bernstein, 1989, 44).

As evidence that not all of the questions have been answered regarding what to disclose to readers of the financial statements, one of the products of the Conceptual Framework project was *Statement of Financial Accounting Concept No. 1* (SFAC 1), "Objectives of Financial Reporting by Business Enterprises." SFAC 1 recognized that there were many different audiences for financial statements and that the external users largely do not have the authority to prescribe what information was disclosed. Disclosure is to a large extent dependent upon management.

SFAC 1 recognized several objectives of financial reporting, of which the following two were most relevant:

1. "Financial reporting should provide information that is useful to present and potential investors and creditors and other users in making rational investment, credit, and similar decisions." (paragraph 34)

2. "Financial reporting should provide information about the economic resources of an enterprise, the

claims to those resources (obligations of the enterprise to transfer resources to other entities and owners'equity),and the effects of transactions, events, and circumstances that change resources and claims to those resources." (paragraph 40)

The first objective would be relevant if the union data being considered for disclosure were found to be related to financial performance. The second objective would be relevant because (1) claims to resources are affected by a union through its pension plan, and any other component of compensation; and (2) because a union election is a "transaction, event, or circumstance" which changes claims to enterprises resources. Spending on research and development may be influenced by the presence of a labor union. Based on these objectives it is argued that union data may meet the objectives of financial reporting and thus fall within the accounting domain. Another statement, SFAC 2, is discussed below. SFAC 2 provided support for specifying the information content of accounting data.

INFORMATION CONTENT FOR DECISION SUPPORT

Statement of Financial Accounting Concept No. 2 (SFAC 2) provided a structure and test for determining when information was useful and needed from an accounting view. This statement was titled "Qualitative Characteristics of Accounting Information" and was issued in 1980.

Two primary qualities of information which enhance its usefulness for decision making purposes are relevance and reliability. Relevance is driven by the predictive value, feedback value, and timeliness of the information. Relevance refers to improving the predictions of decision makers or confirming or correcting a decision maker's earlier expectations (SFAC 2, para. 51). The requirement for predictive value is for value as input for predicting future results, and feedback value refers to the capability to confirm or correct a prediction. Another criteria of accounting information was comparability. If the variables tested proved to differ based on union elections, then it can be argued that this is information which allows the user to make better decisions. These decisions would be based on comparisons, both between firms (union/nonunion) and across time (as unionism increases or decreases).

DATA AVAILABILITY

Data on union elections are reported after the fact by the National Labor Relations Board (NLRB) annually. Material labor stoppages and contract difficulties may, subject to management judgment, be reported to the Securities and Exchange Commission (SEC). Labor elections are reported in the press, at least locally. However, there does not appear to be a uniform mechanism to report these elections in a manner available to the different users of financial statements. As discussed in Chapter III, these data are not immediately usable in the form received from the NLRB, due to editing requirements and use of subsidiary, division, or branch business names. The firms which experience the elections are in the best position to report this data to financial statement users, partly because it may be reported quarterly, and partly because the firms could disclose the information in a uniform and consistent format, if one were available.

PROPOSED DISCLOSURE AND FORMAT

Labor union contracts are executory in nature. This means that the exact persons who will be employed are not specified in the contract, but the terms and conditions of employment are agreed upon. The contract identifies which groups or classifications of employees will be subject to the terms and conditions of the contract. However, since there has been no economic transaction at the time of the election, there is a question of how to recognize the event. It would be possible to compute the present value of the future costs under the labor contract, the same way leases are capitalized, but what would be the debit side of the entry? There would not exist an asset to offset the liability for payment of future labor costs. There is an example available which already is required disclosure material. According to

Statement of Financial Accounting Standard No. 5 (SFAS 5), contingent liabilities (obligations which may exist at a balance sheet date, but depend on uncertain events in the future) are a required disclosure item. Contingent liabilities must be disclosed, either with a dollar amount of loss contingency or a footnote disclosure. A loss contingency must be accrued if the liability is probable at the balance sheet date and the dollar amount of the loss can be reasonably estimated. Under this method, the debit entry is to an expense account and the credit entry is to a liability account. If the chances of the liability actually becoming a loss are not considered probable, but are considered to be either reasonably possible or remote, then no dollar amount is accrued as a loss. Instead the existence of the contingent liability is disclosed in the footnotes to financial statements, along with an estimate of the size range of the liability in dollars.

Because of this issue the suggestion is made that to disclose the data, the information should be placed in the Notes to Financial Statements. These notes are generally identified to specific accounts which appear in the formal statements by inserting a number after the account name. This number refers the reader to the note of the same number. Some explanatory text would be useful to explain that the company had experienced a union election, whether it were a representation or decertification election and whether the union won or lost. This could identify the specific union involved, the percent change in membership due to the election, and the effective date of the change. If this were a representation election wherein the firm were being organized, it would be useful to disclose the length of the contract.

EXISTING DISCLOSURE REQUIREMENTS FOR FINANCIAL REPORTING

Financial statements are one avenue for disclosure of firm data to external users. Generally accepted accounting principles and specific requirements of the Financial Accounting Standards Board and the Securities and Exchange Commission govern the mandatory items which must be disclosed in the annual reports.

There are however many items not included in required disclosures. These items are the difference between the minimum acceptable level of disclosure required in the financial statements and the perfect information set of all data related to the firm which presumably would provide all of the information necessary to make better investment decisions. Existing disclosure requirements for publicly traded firms in the U.S. do not mandate disclosure of a company's relationship with labor unions, length or provisions of current labor contracts, or the extent of unionization within a firm. Disclosure addresses "...relevant financial information both inside and outside the main body of the financial statements themselves..." (Wolk, Francis, and Tearney 1984, 122). Outside the main body of the statements, disclosure categories include (1) supplementary schedules, (2) footnote disclosure, (3) material post-statement date events, (4) forecasts of operations, and (5) management's analysis of operations for the annual report year (Wolk et al. 1984). These categories do not extend to economic environmental conditions (e.g., labor unions) that can affect different firms in different ways over varying time periods. Key to this research was the idea that disclosure of nonfinancial data may be, or may not be, important and useful to users of the firm's financial statements. Wolk et al. noted that "...as the business environment grows more complex, it becomes more difficult to adequately express important financial and operating information within the confines of the traditional financial statements...a considerable body of evidence indicates that capital markets are able rapidly to absorb and reflect new information within security prices." (1984, 122). Under the general rubric of improving the information set available for investment decision making, some prior research supported disclosure of a company's contract with organized labor. This group of research treated the existence of a union as an "environmental variable," which is but one of a number of data items, in addition to the financial statements, which would be useful to investors. Relevant disclosure research is briefly noted here for its relation to the present study, and is reviewed in Chapter II in the survey of related literature.

DISCLOSURE RESEARCH

Before considering the articles on disclosure per se, it may be useful to examine a paper dealing with materiality as a background to the issues of disclosure. Pattillo (1976) examined the influence of political or economic environment conditions on individuals' materiality judgments. That study of the quantitative dimensions of materiality tested the responses to 28 cases requiring materiality judgment made by three knowledgeable audiences of financial executives, bankers, and academics. Among his major findings, Patillo reported that in particular situations, the reader's perception of materiality was influenced by the particular characteristics of the firm and the political and economic environment within which the firm operated: "Varying economic conditions, too, had an impact on the materiality threshold." (30) Labor unions are environmental influences. To organize a company, a union must first win a representation election (to become recognized as the sole bargaining agent for the employees) and then bargain a contract with the employer. Thus it is not possible to predict which company is or will be unionized, even within a given industry. Because of this, the "union variable" (whether employees belong to a union) varies among companies. A company's union status is not a required disclosure item in the annual financial statements according to generally accepted accounting principles. The Securities and Exchange Commission requires publicly traded firms which are subject to the 1933 and 1934 Securities Acts to file various reports with the Commission. Filing these reports is one means of achieving disclosure. There are differences between what is included in the annual financial statements provided to shareholders and the quarterly and annual reports filed with the SEC (an example of this is discussed in Chapter II). Some union data, such as work stoppages or material labor contracts soon to be negotiated, may be disclosed to the SEC through these required reports. Whether this information is disclosed or not is a matter of management judgment. If there is no anticipated difficulty (such as a long strike looming), then the information probably will not be disclosed.

The most likely union data to be disclosed to the SEC are data on labor contracts. According to *Disclosure*[1] labor contract data are included in special circumstances on the Form 10-K annual report, the 8-K and the 20-F. Labor contract data are frequently disclosed on the F-10 and 1933 Act "S" type corporation registration statements. In the 10-K annual report, the only place labor data are required is under the description of business section. Work stoppages or material labor contracts coming due would be reported here if there were some change or difficulty involved. A labor contract signed that year might be discussed in the management and analysis section of the report or in the exhibits to the management discussion. It needs noting that if no changes have occurred or if management does not think them material, nothing will be reported. For firms signing multi-year labor contracts, in the interim years no information will be reported at all about union contracts.   Other union data disclosures are not required at all, anytime. Examples of these would include the name of the union and the number or percent of the company's workforce which belong to it. The 20-F is the equivalent of a 10-K annual report which is required of foreign companies. The 8-K report is required to be filed ten days after a material development, meaning specific events of interest to investors, such as a change of auditors, bankruptcy, mergers and acquisitions, or other material events. Labor contract information may be disclosed on this report under the heading "other material events." There is considerable discretion available to management to decide what to disclose[2]. For all three of these reports there is not a clear requirement to disclose union contract data which is not subject to management discretion and no requirement to disclose additional union data such as that mentioned above.

There are also two registration forms on which labor contract data are frequently reported. These are Form F-10, a combined registration and annual report used by companies for the first two years they are subject to the Securities and Exchange Act of 1934, and "S" type corporations filing registration statements. The next section discusses briefly three relevant studies which provided support for the current research.

Buzby (1974) conducted a test of the extent of disclosure in annual reports by small and medium size firms.   Buzby's intent was to determine both current disclosure levels and to identify any discrepancies in the existing disclosure requirements. He found that compared to what information a group of financial analysts desired in annual reports, on average companies were disclosing only 51 percent of those items.   Some items were reported in the companies' 10-K reports to the SEC, but did not appear in any financial statements. This was cited as an example of "disclosure deficiency."

Support for this book can be found in Buzby's results.   The analysts who provided Buzby with the list of items they wished to see disclosed included two items which were tested in this study.   These are "information pertaining to the company's employee pension plan," and "information about research and development expenditures."

Singhvi and Desai (1971) tested the relationship between disclosure in annual reports and six variables, on a population of 155 industrial firms. They found that there was a direct and significant relationship between rate of return and the extent of corporate disclosure. A similar result was obtained for earnings margin. It is worth mentioning that Singhvi and Desai identified the potential value of variables which were tested in this book. Three items which those authors identified as worthy of disclosure were included in this study: research expenditure amount for the current year, information on labor contracts, and new product development.

Chandra (1974) published a study which identified significant differences in the value of information as viewed by accountants (as preparers of financial statements) and security analysts (as users of the information). Chandra found that accountants did not understand how security analysts valued various information items presented in annual reports. He also found that there were major differences between accountants and analysts regarding the value of the various information items in the reports.

Certain of Chandra's test results support the hypotheses tested in the current study. Chandra found significant differences in the value placed on R&D information between accountants (preparers) and analysts (users). Research and development expenditures was one variable tested in this study. Chandra tested a pension item (material past pension fund liability), but he found no significant difference for this pension item. Pension and retirement spending was another variable tested in this study. Chandra tested one version of productivity, with a question on the value of information on productive capacity and actual output for businesses such as steel mills. Significant differences between accountants and analysts were found for this item. This study tested a different productivity variable, sales per employee.

These articles support the idea that there are disclosure needs of investors which are not completely satisfied. Chandra's research also indicated that the accounting profession has not been completely successful in identifying users' needs for information. That made it possible to identify "environmental factors" which have potential impact on a firm's financial performance measures, but which are not required disclosure items. Labor unions fit this description, as shown by current research on union effects.

RESEARCH ON LABOR UNIONS'
EFFECTS ON FIRMS

Although the unions have been part of the business environment for two hundred years, they have only very recently been recognized as a possible determinant of financial performance. Studies that attempted to identify the key structural variables related to profitability are plentiful if unionization is not considered. Weiss (1974) reviewed 46 different concentration-profit studies, published between 1951 and 1973; none of the studies included a union variable. (Concentration refers to the lack of competition in an industry. Domestic automobile manufacturing, for example, was highly concentrated.)

Union effects on profits and/or performance of firms or industries have been investigated only for the past decade. There is a very limited pool of studies with respect to quantitative firm outcomes and unionization. Four studies which dealt with the disclosure issues and twenty-eight other studies which addressed the relationship between companies and unions are discussed in Chapter II.

That research indicated that labor unions had measurable financial effects on profitability (Clark 1984, Salinger 1984, Karier 1985, Becker and Olson 1992); stock prices (Ruback and Zimmerman 1984, Bronars and Deere 1990); productivity (Brown and Medoff 1978, Clark 1980, Clark 1984, Hirsch and Link 1984, Mitchell and Stone 1992); research and development spending (Connolly, Hirsch, and Hirschey 1986, Allen 1988, Hirsch 1992); and pension benefit costs (Freeman 1981). Thus, it is reasonable to expect that there exist differences in these variables between firms which might be at least partly attributed to their union (or nonunion) status. These papers presented evidence of "union effects" which were attributed to a labor union representing employees. These effects were reflected in a firm's financial statements. No research was found which examined the opposite side of the relationship: what happens to the unionized firm if the union went away (decertification)?

A discussion of the current status of U.S. unions is presented next as an introduction to the research.

LABOR UNIONS - HISTORY AND LEGISLATION

Labor unions have existed in the U.S. since at least 1794, when the Journeymen Cordwainers (Shoemakers) Society of Philadelphia was organized (Merkel 1983, 21). The Cordwainers were perhaps the first labor union to strike against employers, when in 1806 they struck in support of a closed shop and against a wage reduction. "Closed shop" is a union security contract clause which grants the union a certain level of security. A closed shop (employer) clause requires that an individual must be a union member before the employer can offer that person a job (Fossum 1982, 201). The strike resulted in violence done to persons and property, and the employers sued the union on criminal conspiracy charges. These charges were for acting in concert to raise wages and for injuring persons. The union lost the case and the fine bankrupted the union.

Unions have frequently been in an adversarial role to management. Merkel (1983, 29), in discussing the early years of unionism, cited one writer's view of the situation: "In *The Practice of Unionism*, Jack Barbash comments that no political democracy offered unions a more hostile environment than did the United States and that this hostility gave American unionism a character different from any other labor movement." Legislation, mainly as interpreted through court cases, restrained unions and bargaining tactics from 1806 (see the Cordwainers case, above) to the 1930s.

Unions were given landmark federal protection in 1935 with the passage of the National Labor Relations Act (Wagner Act), which specified the rights of employees to engage in union activities: "Employees shall have the right to self-organization, to form, join, or assist labor organizations, to bargain collectively through representatives of their own choosing, and to engage in concerted activities, for the purpose of collective bargaining or other mutual aid or protection." (Section 7) Because of the encouragement given labor unions through this legislation, union growth flourished. By the 1950s, when union growth peaked, one worker in five belonged to a union.

World War II brought government intervention with wage stabilization and machinery for the resolution of disputes (Herman, Kuhn, and Seeber, 1987, 77). The 1950s were a contentious time for unions, with many union officials brought to trial on corruption charges and widespread strike activity. In the face of union corruption and labor unrest, the Taft-Hartley Act was passed as a way of "..."cleaning up" unions without necessarily weakening them." (Herman et al., 78.)

MANAGEMENT'S VIEW OF UNIONS

In the late 1980s and early 1990s, there is still a controversy over unionization, from the viewpoint of business management. Many large firms "...see no realistic likelihood of ever being nonunion again..." (Herman, Kuhn, and Seeber, 1987, 54). Some firms are more candid about their goal of being union-free, as described by Herman, Kuhn, and Seeber's view of the differences between large and small firms with regard to how they view the union:

> "The large corporations have adapted comfortably, if reluctantly, to the institution of unionism, particularly high-technology, capital-intensive corporations to which labor is a small fraction of cost. But smaller employers, particularly in the South and Southwest, bitterly oppose unionization and - in an atmosphere that supports right-to-work laws, which place limitations on union security clauses - have thus far widely succeeded in avoiding it." (53)

If you are an employee of an organization, some of the benefits of your job should be credited to organized labor, whether your employer is unionized or not. As examples these include the 8-hour workday (1917) first won for railroad workers (Fossum 1982, 63); the Labor Day holiday (1882); and company-paid health insurance plans (World War II; Merkel 1983, 165). Wages and benefits obtained by unions tend to be granted also to nonunion workers within the company, or at other companies (Merkel, 166). The major distinction between union and nonunion firms is that in nonunion companies such benefits can be increased, decreased, or completely withdrawn at the company's unilateral decision. In unionized firms, changes must be negotiated with the union. Today members look to the union for other benefits such as job security, retraining, health insurance coverage for retirement, and affordable day care. Today unions are in a state of decline (Fossum, 1982, 503) and membership has slowly and steadily eroded. Table I-1 depicts an 11% drop in the unionized workforce from the highest levels of the 1950s to the current levels. Although

Table I-1. Average percent and number of U.S. labor force unionized, 1950-1979.

Period	Percent Union	Average Annual Employment *	Average Number of Union Employees **
1950-54	34.4%	45,605,000	15,688,000
1955-59	34.6%	49,159,000	17,009,000
1960-64	31.2%	52,767,000	16,463,000
1965-69	29.0%	62,406,000	18,098,000
1970-74	27.2%	70,305,000	19,123,000
1975-79	23.8%	78,962,000	18,793,000

* Net of construction workers.
** Union members as a percentage of average annual employment.
Sources: Total employment and construction: Fossum 1982, 490. Percent union per period: Dickens and Leonard 1985, 326.

the number of people belonging to a union has grown numerically, the percentage of the workforce unionized has declined by about one-third. Many factors likely share responsibility for the decline in membership. Cheap labor overseas has meant the loss of hundreds of thousands of blue collar jobs in manufacturing and textiles; mergers and acquisitions and downsizing have cut jobs in traditional union strongholds; automation such as robotics has reduced demand for some highly skilled manufacturing jobs; and much of the growth in new employment is in areas which are difficult and costly to organize (like small service firms and white collar jobs). Aside from these issues of labor demographics, there are possibly financial reasons for the drop in membership. During the 1970s many unions bargained contracts with cost of living allowances, pay increases, and fringe benefits to try to maintain members' living standards in the face of rapid domestic inflation. Through the 1980s, lower inflation rates meant inflation was not a major concern of union employees. Job security, training, and medical benefits have been bargaining issues instead. Given these concerns many employers have been able to extract significant "give-backs" in recent contract agreements. Give-backs are a reduction in a level of benefits and/or compensation already agreed to in a current or expiring contract. In the new contract period, employees give back something of monetary value in return for greater job security or to help keep the employer competitive or solvent.

For some union members it may seem that their union local is unable to provide much bargaining strength in return for the dues paid. Particularly, this may be an issue for younger employees who desire more current income and less deferred (retirement) benefits, in contrast to the older workers they are replacing. If enough members are dissatisfied with their union, they may petition the National Labor Relations Board to hold a decertification election. In such cases the union which had been elected to represent members in collective bargaining can be decertified as their representative to the employer.

THIS STUDY'S FOCUS

This study examined the changes in several firm performance measures before and after a union election for a selected group of publicly traded firms which had union elections by comparing the results for each observation to the results obtained for a control group of similar firms. The time period tested was January 1978 through December 1989. The control groups used were unique for each observation tested, and were composed of publicly traded firms with the same SIC code, the same fiscal year, which had not had any union election for the entire period of the test.

The purpose of this study was to examine the financial differences that union elections (both representation and decertification) may occasion in publicly traded companies, for purposes of assessing the adequacy of current accounting disclosure requirements regarding labor unions. To do so, four research questions were asked.

Research question 1 asked: were research and development expenditures on a per-employee basis significantly different between firms which had experienced a union election and those which had not?

Research question 2 asked: were pension and retirement expenses on a per-employee basis significantly different between firms which had experienced a union election and those which had not? Research question 3 asked: was profitability significantly different between firms which had experienced a union election and those which had not? Research question 4 asked: was productivity, measured on the basis of sales per employee, significantly different between firms which had experienced a union election and those which had not? These questions were statistically tested for a period of one year prior to the election to one year following the election, and for a period of one year prior to the election to two years after the election. The observations were partitioned into subgroups to examine differences based on election type and outcome.

The dataset was a merged file combining a firm's labor election results with its Compustat financial data on an annual basis. The research design made univariate and multivariate comparisons using pretest/posttest variables between the individual companies and corresponding control groups. The univariate statistical test was a t-test on the differences in the changes between the year before the election and one year following the election, and between one year before the election and two years following the election. A multivariate analysis of variance procedure was performed to determine if the election effects differed for the different types of election outcomes: union wins versus union losses and representation elections versus decertification elections.

OVERVIEW OF SUBSEQUENT CHAPTERS

Following Chapter I's introduction to the research problem, a review of the literature is presented in Chapter II. Exhibit A offers a tabular format summary of the review of the literature. The technical development of the problem, the research methodology employed for testing, and the sources of data are described in Chapter III. Chapter IV presents the results of empirical testing. Chapter V contains the interpretation of the findings, summary, and conclusions along with the significance of the findings and the implications for future research. Limitations of the work are also discussed. Selected references appear at the end.

Notes

1. Personal communication with Disclosure, a source of public company information and publisher of *Compact Disclosure*, March 6, 1991.

2. Personal communication with Mr. Richard Reinhard, Office of the Chief Accountant, Securities and Exchange Commission, March 6, 1991.

II

Survey Of Related Literature

Literature germane to the issue of union effects was divided into several groups. The first dealt with whether there might be useful data in union existence which should be disclosed to enhance accounting information content. There was a fairly small body of relevant disclosure literature. The remaining articles were grouped by their focus on specific (mainly financial) attributes, including productivity, stock price effects, compensation, or research and development expenditures.

DISCLOSURE

Information was sparse with respect to disclosure of particular items of a firm's characteristics. One study which did comment on disclosure of political or economic environment influences on a particular company was Pattillo (1976). This study examined whether a company's disclosure of political or economic environment influences had any effect on the judgments made by informed readers of the financial statements. Pattillo's study of the quantitative dimensions of materiality tested the responses to 28 cases requiring materiality judgments made by three knowledgeable audiences. Six hundred and eighty-four persons took part in the test. These were financial executives from Fortune 500 or medium-sized companies (as financial statement preparers), bankers and analysts (as accounting information users), and academics. Among Pattillo's major findings, it was reported that "varying economic conditions, too, had an impact on the materiality threshold." (30)

Labor unions are environmental influences. To organize a company, a labor union must win a representation election, and then bargain a contract with the employer. Thus, it was not possible to predict which company is or will be unionized, even within a given industry. Because of this, the "union variable" (whether the company's employees belong to a union or not) varied among companies. A company's union status is not a required disclosure item. Buzby (1974) tested a sample of 88 small and medium size firms' annual reports against a list of 38 possible disclosure items. The purpose was to measure, for each item, the extent of disclosure and any relationship between "importance" and disclosure. Overall the work might also point to discrepancies in the existing disclosure requirements.

The Buzby study used a matched pairs design. To obtain the total 88 firms tested, two samples of 44 small and medium-sized firms each were matched on size (total assets net of accumulated depreciation), three-digit SIC codes, and fiscal year-ends. The sample of the first 44 companies was obtained by listing all companies in the 1971 *Moody's OTC Industrial Manual* and "every fourth company listed in the OTC quotation section of the March 13, 1972 issue of the *Wall Street Journal*." (428) This amounted to 200 firms. Selection of the 44 firms was not random. For the first sample, selection from the list of 200 possible firms required that there be available "a suitable match" of a firm whose common stock was traded on the AMEX or NYSE. The resulting test sample included firms in 22 industries, with fiscal years ending between June 30, 1970 and June 30, 1971. The 88 firms' assets ranged from 149.5 million to 2.9 million dollars. The mean asset size was 37.2 million dollars.

The test instrument was a survey questionnaire containing 39 different disclosure items. This was based on work done by Alan Cerf in *Corporate Reporting and Investment Decisions* (1961). The questionnaire was mailed to 500 professional financial analysts. A copy of the test instrument and the results obtained is shown in Figure II-1. Survey respondents rated each disclosure item on a scale of zero to four, with a four assigned to items which were considered essential in an annual report. A zero was given to items not considered necessary in the annual statements. One item was unscorable. For the remaining 38 items the author developed a weighting scale, to indicate each item's usefulness and desirability in an annual report, based on the scores provided by survey respondents. For each of the 88 annual reports a worksheet was completed to measure the extent of disclosure for the 38 items. Each item was given a weighted score. Certain items were crosschecked from the annual report to the SEC 10-K filing.

	Weight (0-4)
1. Information on company directors, such as their names and major outside affiliations.	2.93
2. Information on management, such as their names, ages, and functional responsibilities.	3.23
3. Forecast of next year's earnings per share.	1.61
4. Allowance for doubtful accounts.	3.09
5. Breakdown of inventories into raw materials, goods-in-process and finished goods.	3.03
6. Method used to determine the cost of inventories: e.g., LIFO, FIFO, etc.; and, the basis for valuing inventories: e.g., lower of cost or market.	3.64
7. Description of major plants and warehouses, including location, function and size.	2.09
8. Description of major products produced, including an indication of those products that are new.	3.37
9. Information about the firm's stock option plan.	2.69
10. Dollar value of the firm's order backlog.	3.33
11. Breakdown of tangible assets into a form such as land, equipment, and buildings.	3.19
12. Indication of the original cost, accumulated depreciation and the current amount of depreciation charged to income for the tangible assets.	3.57
13. Specification of the method used to compute depreciation.	3.71
14. Information about consolidated and unconsolidated subsidiaries such as percentage ownership, dividends received, equity in undistributed earnings and summary financial statements.	3.71
15. Pertinent information about investments in firms not qualifying as subsidiaries such as cost and market value of the investment, percentage ownership, dividends received and equity in undistributed earnings.	3.49
16. Information about the leasing of assets (firm is the lessee).	3.40
17. Information pertaining to the company's employee pension plan.	2.88
18. Current market value for marketable securities.	2.62
19. Dollar value of the firm's capital expenditures.	3.80
20. Budgeted capital expenditures for the coming year.	3.50

	Weight (0-4)
21. Discussion of the major factors which will influence next year's results to include an indication of the firm's relationship to its industry and the economy..	3.23
22. Measure of the physical level of output such as the percentage of plant capacity utilized..	3.11
23. Number of employees...	2.82
24. Information on the effects of changing price levels, such as pertinent price indices or supplementary price level adjusted statements............	2.90
25. Information about research and development expenditures.............	3.28
26. Number of stockholders...	2.11
27. Maintenance and repair expenditures.............................	2.37
28. Breakdown of sales revenue by major product lines and customer classes.......	3.67
29. Breakdown of operating earnings by major product lines and customer classes......	3.75
30. Indication of sales revenue and net income attributable to foreign operations......	3.77
31. Historical summary of important operating data....................	3.77
How many years should be covered by the summary?_____ (indicate no. of years)	
32. Indication of employee morale such as the rate of absenteeism, turnover, etc.....	1.58
33. Information on business combinations such as the accounting method used to record the combination, prices paid, method of payment, accounting treatment of goodwill, etc..	3.40
34. Schedule of interest and principal due on long-term debt in future years.......	3.38
35. Information pertaining to changes in accounting methods.............	3.87
36. Statement of sources and uses of funds..........................	3.69
37. Explanation (reconciliation) of the calculation of primary and fully diluted earnings per share..	3.58
38. Information on deferred taxes: e.g., reconciliation of the amount charged to income and the amount actually paid................................	3.42
39. Statement of company objectives and dividend policy...............	2.72

Buzby's weights for each item are shown in Figure II-1. The author noted that "The overall mean extent of disclosure was equal to 51.2%" (432). This was an indication of "extensive opportunity" to expand extent of disclosure. Some items were reported in all 88 10-Ks but not reported in any financial statements (432), so this is an example of "disclosure deficiency."

Support for the present research was found in Buzby's results. Item 17 (see Figure II-1), "Information pertaining to the company's employee pension plan," was rated at 2.88 of a possible four for being essential in an annual report. Item 25, "Information about research and development expenditures" was rated at 3.28 of a possible four. These two disclosure items were directly tested in this study.

Singhvi and Desai (1971) conducted an empirical test of the relationship between disclosure (in annual reports) and six variables using a sample of 155 industrial firms. The sample of annual reports used came from 100 listed firms and 55 unlisted (OTC) firms with year-ends between April 1, 1965 and March 31, 1966. Listed corporations were randomly chosen from the 1965 Fortune directory of the 500 largest industrial corporations in the U.S. Unlisted firms were selected by a sampling of the 800 corporations listed in the *New York Times* national over-the-counter-quotations. One hundred firms were selected and asked by letter for a copy of their annual reports; 55 complied.

The dependent variable was a calculated score termed the "index of disclosure." This number was regressed against the six independent variables described below in the regression model. Both multivariate linear regression and stepwise regression were performed. Based on earlier work by Cerf (1961), 34 representative items which could be disclosed by a firm in its financial statements were listed and each item was given a weighted score of points ranging from 1 to 4. The total of all possible weights was 68. The Index of Disclosure is reproduced as Figure II-2. For each firm in the sample, the authors rated the 34 disclosure items, assigning points to each firm. This score was the dependent variable, termed the index of disclosure, which was used in regression analysis.

The multivariate linear regression model was

$$I = 30.90 + 0.70(A) + 0.0060(N) + 8.10(L) + 2.21(C) - 0.03(R) + 0.25(E),$$

where:

I = index of quality of disclosure
A = total assets in billions of dollars
N = number of stockholders in thousands
L = stock exchange listing status (1=listed, 0=OTC)
C = auditing CPA firm (1=big eight; 0=non-big-eight)
R = rate of return (net profit to net worth) as a percent
E = earnings margin in percentage (ratio of net profit to net sales)

Testing resulted in a coefficient of multiple determination (R squared) of 0.43442.

The results obtained by Singhvi and Desai included six items. (1) They found a positive and significant relationship (at the 0.01 level with a Chi-Square test) between asset size and mean disclosure score. (2) They found a positive relationship between quality of disclosure and number of stockholders. (3) They found a positive relationship between listing status and quality of disclosure. Singhvi and Desai noted that the NYSE has the highest disclosure requirements, and NASD has the lowest, since NASD did not specify the contents of the financial statements (only that a financial statement must have been provided). In addition, (4) CPA firm size was found to influence the quality of disclosure. The mean disclosure score of 133 firms audited by "large" CPA firms (ie, big-eights) was 40.43. Firms audited by "small" CPA firms (all non-big-eights) obtained a mean disclosure score of 36.38. This difference was significant at the 0.01 level.

Figure II-2. Index of Disclosure (Source: Singhvi and Desai 1971, 138)

Items of Information	Weight
1. Comparative Income Statement for 2 years	4
2. Comparative Balance Sheet for 2 years	4
3. Statement of reconciliation of earned surplus	3
4. Statement of cash-flow (or source and application	3
5. Summary of important financial statistics: 10 years =3 points 6-9 years=2 points 4-5 years=1 point	3
6. Method of inventory valuation	1
7. Basis of inventory valuation	2
7. Sales breakdown by division or by individual companies in a consolidated statement	3
8. Method of depreciation	3
9. Description of type of capital expenditure planned	3
10. Capital expenditure amount for current year	3
11. Research expenditure amount for current year	3
12. Statement of gross and net property accounts	2
13. Sales broken down by customer or industry served	2
14. Sales separated by major product lines	2

Items of Information	Weight
15. Discussion of major factors affecting future business	2
16. Information on labor contracts	2
17. Basic policies and objectives of management	2
18. Description of principal plants	2
19. Details of outstanding stock issues	1
20. Index of selling prices	1
21. Index of raw material prices	1
22. Discussion of new product development	1
23. Discussion of industry trends	1
24. Number of employees	1
25. Description of management	1
26. List of names of directors	1
27. Summary of major products produced	1
28. Information on tax clearances & pending tax claims	1
29. Advertising expenses for current year	2
30. Contingent liabilities	2
31. Inventory breakdown	2
32. Sources of other earnings	1
33. Backlogs and projections	1
34. Number of stockholders	1
	--
Total number of weights	68

(5) Rate of return also influenced the score on the disclosure index. As the rate of return increased, disclosure increased. However, when rate of return was 20 percent or greater, the disclosure index decreased. Their results are reproduced below in Table II-1.

Singhvi and Desai tested this by examining 10 listed and 10 nonlisted firms with 20 percent or more rate of return. They found that a majority of these 20 firms obtained the bulk of their financing internally (from retained earnings) as opposed to issuing new common equity. Since these firms did not access the equity market as

Table II-1. Rate of return and quality of disclosure.

Rate of Return	All Corporations		Listed Corporations		Unlisted Corporations	
(in percent)	n	$\bar{x}$	n	$\bar{x}$	n	$\bar{x}$
Loss to less than 10	46	38.7	29	42.9	17	31.6
10-15	56	40.1	41	43.0	15	32.2
15-20	33	42.0	20	44.7	13	38.0
20 and up	20	37.2	10	40.9	10	33.6
Total	155		100		55	

(Results significant at 0.02 level with Chi-Square test. Source: Singhvi and Desai 1971, 134, Table 5.)

frequently as the other firms, perhaps they gave "less attention to the needs of the investing public in connection with disclosing information" (1971, 134). (6) Similar to the results found for rate of return, as the earnings margin increased, so did the quality of disclosure. However, when the earnings margin exceeded ten percent, the disclosure index fell, for both listed and unlisted corporations. These results are reproduced below in Table II-2.

Stepwise regression was also performed to indicate the relative importance of each of the six variables to the R squared of the regression model. The order of entrance into the regression indicated explanatory power, with the first variable selected being the most important. In order, the variables selected were listing status, asset size, CPA firm, earnings margin, number of stockholders, and rate of return.

It is worth mentioning that Singhvi and Desai identified the potential value of variables which were tested in this study. There are three items identified by Singhvi and Desai as worthy of disclosure: research expenditure amount for current year (no. 11) which received a weight of three; information on labor contracts (no. 16) with a weight of two; and discussion of new product development (no. 22) with a weight of one. In the present study, research and development spending was one dependent variable tested in changing union environments. Information on labor contracts was the logical next step following data on union elections. Union elections were the independent variable in this study.

Table II-2. Earnings margin and quality of disclosure.

Rate of Return (in percent)	All Corporations		Listed Corporations		Unlisted Corporations	
	n	$\bar{x}$	n	$\bar{x}$	n	$\bar{x}$
Loss to less than 2.5	17	36.0	9	40.6	8	30.9
2.5 to 5	36	39.0	22	42.3	14	33.6
5 to 7.5	46	40.4	33	42.6	13	34.9
7.5 to 10	29	41.8	19	45.6	10	34.4
10 and up	27	39.9	17	43.4	10	33.7
Total	155		100		55	

(Results significant at 0.05 level with Chi-Square test. Source: Singhvi and Desai 1971, 135, Table 6.)

The next study, by Chandra (1974), found that even when information items were disclosed, at least one of the professional groups for whom the statements were intended had significantly different perceptions of the value of the disclosures. Chandra (1974) performed a study which showed there were significant differences "between the value of information to security analysts as perceived by accountants and the value of information to security analysts...for equity investment decisions" (737). The subjects chosen at random to receive a mailed questionnaire survey included 600 certified public accountants (CPAs) at big-eight accounting firms and 400 chartered financial analysts (CFAs). The response rate was 49.8 percent.

The survey instrument contained 58 disclosure items which were intended to be representative of data used for equity investment decisions. Items included were selected for general significance, availability, and frequency of use. These items were in six categories: 1) balance sheet items, 2) items from the income statement and the statement of retained earnings, 3) other statement items, 4) items derived from data in the statements (trends and ratios), 5) accounting method data, and 6) projections and budgets.

Three subject samples were used. The first group of CPAs (group A) rated the 58 information items in the questionnaire (shown in Figure II-3) on a five-point scale, with 5 being "very important" for equity investment decisions, and 1 meaning "very unimportant." Group A's rating was based on their perception of the value of each item to security analysts for common stock investment decisions. The second group (B) of CPAs rated the questionnaire items as they themselves valued the information for common stock investment decisions. The third group (C) of CFAs (security analysts) rated the items as they valued the information for equity investment decisions. Three hypotheses were tested, using a t-test with alpha equal to 0.05 to detect significant differences. The hypotheses were:

> "H1:   There is no significant difference
> between the value of information to security
> analysts as perceived by accountants (Subject
> group A) and the value of information to
> security analysts (Subject group C) for
> equity investment decisions.
> H2:   There is no significance difference
> between the accountants (Subject group B)
> and the security analysts (Subject group C)

Information Items	Mean of Responses Subject Group			T Statistics (Probability)		
	A	B	C	H_1 (A:C)	H_2 (B:C)	H_3 (A:B)
I. Balance Sheet Items						
1. Total assets reported, end of period (e.o.p.).	4.226	4.107	4.291	0.692 (.491)	1.711 (.087)	1.105 (.271)
2. Total current assets reported, e.o.p.	4.648	4.572	4.589	0.818 (.412)	0.245 (.810)	1.140 (.254)
3. Total current liabilities, e.o.p.	4.642	4.591	4.622	0.305 (.764)	0.495 (.624)	0.751 (.452)
4. Cost of marketable securities, e.o.p.	4.000	3.994	3.928	0.668 (.504)	0.644 (.522)	0.081 (.934)
5. Market value of marketable securities, e.o.p.	4.497	4.437	4.289	2.408 (.016)	1.806 (.072)	0.760 (.448)
6. Amount of inventory reported and the method used in its valuation, e.o.p.	4.415	4.314	4.494	1.127 (.264)	2.575 (.012)	1.342 (.188)
7. Breakdown of inventory reported under major categories, e.o.p.	3.563	3.396	3.944	3.842 (.002)	5.633 (.000)	1.575 (.114)
8. Fifo cost of inventory, e.o.p.	3.620	3.465	3.828	1.891 (.060)	3.417 (.002)	1.359 (.174)
9. Market value of inventory, e.o.p.	3.191	3.241	3.861	6.241 (.000)	5.885 (.000)	0.420 (.674)
10. Amount of past pension fund liability, if material, e.o.p.	3.811	3.642	4.033	2.192 (.030)	3.906 (.002)	1.558 (.118)
11. Amount of goodwill recognized in each acquisition completed during the period.	4.472	4.440	4.478	0.125 (.904)	0.508 (.610)	0.402 (.690)
12. Amount of deferred income tax liability or prepaid income tax, e.o.p.	4.245	4.233	4.367	1.431 (.152)	1.561 (.118)	0.171 (.866)
13. Investment in each subsidiary co., e.o.p.	3.314	3.226	3.983	6.437 (.000)	7.539 (.000)	0.724 (.472)

Information Items	Mean of Responses Subject Group			T Statistics (Probability)		
	A	B	C	H_1 (A:C)	H_2 (B:C)	H_3 (A:B)
14. Minority interest reported in each consolidated subsidiary, e.o.p.	3.245	3.151	3.833	5.441 (.000)	6.544 (.000)	0.785 (.436)
15. Reported capital expenditures (additions to physical facilities), for the period (f.t.p.)	3.747	3.692	4.483	10.291 (.000)	10.275 (.000)	0.645 (.522)
16. Total common shareholders' equity and number of common shares outstanding, e.o.p.	4.384	4.333	4.678	4.305 (.001)	4.614 (.000)	0.593 (.556)
17. Number of stock warrants and convertible securities outstanding, e.o.p.	4.440	4.472	4.661	3.133 (.002)	2.895 (.004)	0.428 (.668)
18. Amount and breakdown of preferred stock and long-term debt by type, dividend and interest rate and maturity, e.o.p.	4.182	4.151	4.300	1.432 (.154)	1.752 (.102)	0.379 (.704)
II. Income Statement and Statement of Retained Earnings Items						
19. Amount of revenue and the method used in its recognition (e.g., franchise business, construction firms, etc.), f.t.p.	4.824	4.867	4.867	1.023 (.308)	0.214 (.834)	0.996 (.318)
20. Operating income reported (before nonrecurring gains and losses), f.t.p.	4.887	4.811	4.839	1.255 (.208)	0.628 (.528)	1.771 (.078)
21. Amount and breakdown of operating expenses reported, f.t.p.	4.126	3.975	4.650	7.210 (.000)	8.613 (.000)	1.604 (.110)
22. Cost of goods sold reported, f.t.p.	4.358	4.264	4.503	1.891 (.038)	2.997 (.004)	1.145 (.250)

Figure II-3. The value of information items between accountants and security analysts (Source: Chandra 1974, 738-740) 3 of 7

Information Items	Mean of Responses Subject Group			T Statistics (Probability)		
	A	B	C	H_1 (A:C)	H_2 (B:C)	H_3 (A:B)
23. Amount of depreciation reported and the method used in its computation, f.t.p.	4.308	4.189	4.683	5.296 (.002)	7.283 (.000)	1.446 (.148)
24. Amount of straightline depreciation on long-lived assets, e.o.p.	3.270	3.127	4.011	7.449 (.000)	9.129 (.000)	1.402 (.162)
25. Amount of accelerated depreciation on long-lived assets, f.t.p.	3.389	3.239	4.117	7.348 (.000)	9.488 (.000)	1.489 (.136)
26. Amount of nonrecurring gains and losses reported, f.t.p.	4.692	4.660	4.711	0.370 (.712)	0.928 (.352)	0.529 (.596)
27. Amount expended on human resources (e.g., hiring, training, etc.), if material, f.t.p.	2.792	2.843	3.206	4.067 (.002)	3.667 (.002)	0.476 (.632)
28. Amount expended on research and development and exploration, f.t.p.	4.050	4.038	4.411	4.427 (.002)	5.279 (.002)	0.172 (.866)
29. Amount expended on advertising and publicity, f.t.p.	3.038	2.994	3.683	6.668 (.000)	7.192 (.000)	0.428 (.668)
30. Amount of goodwill and other intangibles amortised, if material, f.t.p.	4.453	4.302	4.517	0.851 (.396)	0.015 (.004)	2.033 (.044)
31. Amount of income tax expense, f.t.p.	4.547	4.459	4.644	1.457 (.142)	2.565 (.010)	1.205 (.230)
32. Amount of each subsidiary's earnings and parent co.'s share of its earnings, f.t.p.	3.610	3.528	4.383	7.404 (.000)	7.986 (.000)	0.631 (.528)
33. Rent payments or receipts on long-term leases, f.t.p.	3.648	3.447	4.044	4.472 (.000)	6.292 (.000)	2.070 (.038)

Information Items	Mean of Responses Subject Group			T Statistics (Probability)		
	A	B	C	H_1 (A:C)	H_2 (B:C)	H_3 (A:B)
III. Other Statements						
34. Source and application of funds statements, f.t.p.	4.384	4.327	4.644	3.820 (.002)	4.204 (.000)	0.646 (.522)
35. Price level adjusted annual corporate reports as supplementary statements	3.019	3.101	2.943	0.641 (.522)	1.279 (.202)	0.681 (.496)
IV. Ratios, Statistics, and Details of Information						
36. Earnings per share reported, f.t.p., and the method used in its computation	4.836	4.736	4.888	1.357 (.174)	2.992 (.004)	1.852 (.064)
37. Compounded rate of growth in earnings per share for the last five to ten years	3.786	3.811	3.622	1.512 (.132)	1.755 (.082)	0.236 (.810)
38. Dividend per share on common shares, f.t.p.	4.340	4.264	4.306	0.433 (.668)	0.518 (.604)	0.943 (.348)
39. Breakdown of sales, income after tax and investment by continent or hemisphere (where international operations contribute over 15% of co's. revenues, f.t.p.)	3.755	3.667	4.239	5.144 (.000)	5.874 (.000)	0.866 (.386)
40. Breakdown of sales, net operating income and investment of diversified co's. by operating division, product, line of business, or customer group (segmented on the basis of 15% or more contribution to gross revenue or operating income, f.t.p.)	4.138	4.006	4.648	7.053 (.000)	7.637 (.000)	1.338 (.182)

Figure II-3. The value of information items between accountants and security analysts
(Source: Chandra 1974, 738-740) 5 of 7

Information Items	Mean of Responses Subject Group			T Statistics (Probability)		
	A	B	C	H_1 (A:C)	H_2 (B:C)	H_3 (A:B)
41. Terms, annual rentals and breakdown of long term leases by the type of property leased (e.g., real estate, equipment, etc.) e.o.p.	3.365	3.409	3.667	2.917 (.004)	2.545 (.012)	0.400 (.690)
42. Backlog and projection of orders, e.o.p.	3.950	4.063	4.433	5.831 (.000)	4.664 (.000)	1.196 (.234)
43. Productive capacity and actual output (e.g., steel mills, oil co's, etc.), f.t.p.	3.755	3.906	4.378	7.257 (.000)	5.662 (.000)	1.649 (.100)
44. Extent of dependence on a few customers (e.g., defense contracts, foreign markets, etc.).	4.428	4.522	4.575	2.068 (.040)	0.835 (.406)	1.240 (.216)
45. Share of market in major product areas, f.t.p.	3.778	3.849	4.263	5.684 (.000)	4.907 (.000)	0.767 (.442)
46. Number and type of common shareholders (e.g., individuals, institutions, etc.), e.o.p.	3.189	3.164	3.278	0.792 (.430)	1.009 (.314)	0.211 (.834)
47. Number of shares in the company owned by its officers, e.o.p.	3.780	3.711	3.828	0.578 (.562)	1.352 (.178)	0.779 (.436)
48. Terms of stock option plan and shares involved, e.o.p.	4.119	4.069	3.817	3.528 (.002)	3.149 (.002)	0.620 (.536)
49. Contractual restrictions on common dividend, if any, e.o.p.	4.365	4.392	4.139	2.722 (.007)	2.963 (.004)	0.386 (.704)
50. Names of top executives, lines of authority and their remuneration	3.327	3.191	3.753	4.043 (.000)	5.358 (.000)	1.184 (.238)

Information Items	Mean of Responses Subject Group			T Statistics (Probability)		
	A	B	C	H_1 (A:C)	H_2 (B:C)	H_3 (A:B)
V. Accounting Method						
51. Accounting method followed for research and development, and exploration costs.	4.365	4.283	4.467	1.281 (.202)	2.331 (.020)	1.082 (.280)
52. Accounting method followed for advertising and publicity costs.	3.152	3.132	3.617	4.258 (.000)	4.481 (.000)	0.181 (.858)
53. Accounting method (purchase vs. pooling) followed for each acquisition and merger completed during the period.	4.823	4.792	4.772	0.972 (.332)	0.378 (.704)	0.599 (.556)
54. Method followed for reporting long term leases, f.t.p.	3.874	3.874	4.117	2.686 (.008)	2.597 (.010)	0.072 (.946)
VI. Projections and Budgetary Disclosure						
55. Planned capital expenditure for next twelve months.	3.579	3.597	4.356	10.171 (.000)	10.125 (.000)	0.219 (.826)
56. Planned expenditure on research and development and exploration for next twelve months.	3.478	3.648	4.117	7.293 (.000)	5.581 (.000)	1.858 (.064)
57. Planned expenditure on advertising and publicity for next twelve months.	2.981	3.019	3.472	5.062 (.000)	4.540 (.000)	0.372 (.712)
58. Cash flow projections for next two to five years.	3.329	3.434	4.067	6.831 (.000)	6.105 (.000)	0.954 (.342)
Number of Significant Differences at 5%				35	40	2

Figure II-3. The value of information items between accountants and security analysts
(Source: Chandra 1974, 738-740) 7 of 7

NOTES

1. Degrees of freedom: H_1 and H_2: 337; H_3:316.
2. (0.000) as probability for the three hypotheses indicates a probability of less than 0.001.
3. Subject Group A: Accountants as they perceive the value of information for equity investment decisions to security analysts.

   Subject Group B: Accountants as they rate the value of information for equity investment decision.

   Subject Group C: Security analysts as they rate the value of information for equity investment decisions.

on the value of information for equity
investment decisions.

H3:   There is no significant difference
between the value of information to security
analysts as perceived by accountants (Subject
Group A) and the value of information to
accountants (Subject Group B) for equity
investment decisions. " (Chandra, 1974, 735)

The first hypothesis, which tested whether accountants understood
how security analysts valued the information, was rejected for 35 of 58
items.   The second hypothesis, stating no difference existed between
accountants and security analysts on the value of information, was
rejected 40 of 58 times.   The last hypothesis showed little difference in
accountants' value placed on information with respect to their different
roles as preparers and users of financial information.   For this test the
null hypothesis was rejected for only two items.

Chandra's results for the first two hypotheses were quite similar.
For the first hypothesis there were clearly significant differences in the
way preparers of financial statements and users of financial statements
valued the same information items disclosed in an annual report.   The
second hypothesis obtained just as convincing a difference in how
accountants and analysts valued information to make the same decision
on equity investment.

Certain of the test results supported the hypotheses tested in this
study.   Research and development expenditures was one variable tested
in this study.   Chandra found significant differences in the value placed
on R&D information between accountants (preparers) and analysts
(users) as specified by these two items: Item 28, Amount expended on
research and development and exploration; and item 56, Planned
expenditure on research and development and exploration for the next
twelve months.   However, the method of accounting for R&D and
exploration (item 51) was not valued differently by the two subject
groups.   Pension and retirement spending was another variable tested
in this study.   Chandra had one related item (number 10) regarding
material past pension fund liability, and there was no significant
difference found on this item.   One question concerned productivity.
Item 43 questioned the value of information on productive capacity and
actual output for businesses such as steel mills.   Significant differences
were found for this item.   This study tested for a different productivity

variable, sales per employee. Generally Chandra found, for all variables that were valued differently, that analysts placed a higher value on those items than did the accountants.

These articles support the idea that there are disclosure needs of investors which are not completely satisfied. Chandra's research also indicated that the accounting profession has not been completely successful in identifying users' needs for information. Therefore it is possible to identify "environmental factors" which have potential impact on a firm's financial performance measures, but which are not required disclosure items. Labor unions fit this description. The next group of articles was concerned with union effects on productivity.

PRODUCTIVITY

Studies of relationships between unionism and productivity either used databases of industries, disaggregated at SIC levels, or firm level databases.

Brown and Medoff (1978), in an industry-level examination of 20 two-digit SIC code manufacturing industries, tested productivity levels in union and nonunion establishments. When productivity was defined as value added divided by labor cost, they found productivity in unionized establishments was 24 percent higher than in nonunion establishments. Confirmation testing using value of shipments as the alternate dependent variable also resulted in a similar (21 percent) higher unionized productivity level. Brown and Medoff found that the productivity increase was approximately offset by increased wages paid to union members, so that the two effects largely cancelled each other.

Clark (1980), in a case study of the cement industry, examined the impact of unionization in six cement plants which were unionized between 1953 and 1976. That study used multiple union dichotomous variables: one for the year the local union was chartered and another each year subsequent to the year of chartering. Because the study dealt with a single industry producing a homogenous product, it eliminated any differences due to changes in technology. Output was measured in physical units (tons of cement per manhour). Clark found that unionization resulted in a six to eight percent increase in productivity and a 12 to 18 percent increase in wages (468). Clark noted that with labor's share approximating .43, overall unit costs would increase five to eight percent. Since the productivity effect was six to eight percent, unionization had no net effect on unit costs.

In a later study, Clark (1984) used the PIMS dataset (Profit Impact of Market Strategies). He found union firms were one percent more productive (in value added per employee) than nonunion firms.

Hirsch and Link (1984) examined 19 two-digit SIC industries with data for 1957-1973. The dependent variable was the average annual rate of growth in total factor productivity. Using R&D, concentration ratios (lack of competition in an industry), percent of sales to the private sector, and an index of the cyclical instability of industry output as control variables, the authors found that annual productivity growth was 3.6 percent to 4.4 percent slower under unionism (Table 1, 35).

Allen (1988) tested 74 three- and four-digit SIC manufacturing industries for growth in labor productivity indices which are published by the Department of Labor. That paper was noteworthy because the output measures were based on physical quantities produced, meaning the data should have been reasonably accurate. Research and development, concentration ratios, and unionization were the independent regression variables. Allen found that productivity increased "slightly faster in industries with high initial levels of unionization and markedly faster in industries where percentage union is declining most rapidly..."(104). The regression coefficients for both cases were, however, not significant.

Link (1981), in a study of 51 companies in seven industries, found annual productivity growth was 2.5 percent slower under unionism. In a later study, Link (1982) used a sample of 97 manufacturing firms in chemicals, machinery, and petroleum with data from 1975-1979. In those firms which appeared to be heavily unionized, productivity growth was 9 to 10 percent slower than in nonunionized firms. Link's research differs from the previously discussed papers in that Link used data on specific companies, in contrast to research which used mainly industry-level data.

Mitchell and Stone (1992) surveyed domestic sawmills for 1986, using a standardized product (lumber) to determine whether unionized sawmills were more productive than nonunion sawmills. Productivity was measured as board feet of lumber produced, controlling for quality of output and consumption of inputs. The sample included 46 union and 37 nonunion mills. The authors found that unionized sawmills were significantly less productive (12 to 21 percent less) than sawmills which were not organized. It was suggested the difference was partially due to incentive pay systems in nonunion sawmills, or to increased flexibility of nonunion mills' workforces, wherein absenteeism would be less of a drain on productivity.

There appears to be no clear evidence as to either the magnitude or sign of union-induced productivity differences. Hirsch and Link (35) suggested that changes in unionization levels may bring asymmetrical effects.

STOCK PRICES

Greer, Martin, and Reusser (1980) tested a sample of 91 large strikes occurring from 1951 to 1973 for effects on shareholder wealth. The strike data came from *Analysis of Work Stoppages* published by the Bureau of Labor Statistics. This source identified strikes in firms with a minimum of 10,000 employees. The sample contained 91 strikes at 65 firms for which CRSP monthly data for price, dividends, and market return were available for the period 1951-1973. The sample excluded any firm with multiple strikes less than 36 months apart.

Their study used regression analysis to calculate expected monthly returns for firms in the sample, which were then compared to the actual monthly returns. The return was defined as $R_j = (P_t - P_{t-1} + D_t)/P_{-1}$, where:

R_j = the return on the jth stock,
P_t = the end-of-period stock price,
P_{-1} = the stock price at the end of the period t-1, and
D_t = period t's dividend.

The capital asset pricing model was used to estimate the expected return for each stock:

$$E(R_j) = R_f + B[E(r_m) - R_f,$$

where:

R_f = riskless rate of return,
$E(r_m)$ = expected return on a market portfolio, and
B = firm's Beta coefficient.

Actual monthly returns were calculated from the Center for Research in Security Prices (CRSP) monthly data files. Abnormal returns were calculated as the actual return minus the expected return:

$$R^a_{jt} = R_{jt} - E(R_{jt}).$$

R^a was a linear regression residual. The authors argued that were strikes to adversely affect returns, the residuals ought to be negative. If the means of a large sample were approximately zero, strikes would have no effect on returns; if the means were positive, then strikes affected returns in a positive manner (220).

A test period of 30 months either side of the strike's beginning was used. The sample was divided into three subsets. The first group contained 27 strikes lasting from one to ten days; the second group contained 28 strikes lasting 11 to 29 days had 28 strikes, and the last group contained 36 strikes of 30 days or longer.

The results of the regressions yielded an average R^2 of .34, but the cumulative average residuals behaved differently for each of the three subsets. For the shortest strikes, the cumulative average residuals were below the market to begin with (30 months prior to the strike), declined before the strike began, and fell further post-strike, to a low of -0.13 some 22 months after the strike. The authors suggested these were weak firms unable to bear long strikes. For the 11 to 29 day strike group, the cumulative average residual was at the market level but increased following the strike. Residuals for this group peaked at +0.10 approximately 16 months after the strike, possibly in recognition of management winning the dispute. For strikes of 30 days or more, the cumulative average residuals were above market at the beginning of the test period. They rose to a peak of +0.17 just prior to the strike, but declined steadily to -0.05 some 25 months after the strike. The authors suggested that this behavior represented firms with returns greater than the market return which had been targeted by the union (for a share of perceived high profits). Such firms would be better able to withstand longer strikes. Shareholders, however, did not view long strikes as beneficial to them, so the residuals declined.

Neumann (1980) tested labor strike effects on firms' daily stock prices. A nonrandom sample of 340 firms was obtained by reviewing the *Wall Street Journal Index* for references to strikes, with a requirement that a firm be listed on the New York Stock Exchange. The article was then reviewed to determine if the strike's starting and ending dates were given. If only the starting date was available, the observation was used solely for prestrike analysis. If no starting date was given the observation was dropped. The period covered was 1967-1975, excluding 1972-73 due to wage-price controls. Industry-wide strikes and multi-employer bargaining unit strikes were excluded from the sample. Neumann computed excess return data for both the announcement of a strike and the conclusion of a strike, with daily data beginning 14 days before and ending 14 days after each event. Abnormal returns were calculated for each firm, using the method described earlier (Greer et al. 1980).

Neumann found a negative abnormal return on the date a strike was announced of .44 percent, and a positive abnormal return of .29 percent when the strike ended. (The daily return would have been on the order of .049 percent to obtain an annualized 20 percent return. Thus the excess return on the day of the strike was about ten times the average daily return and was also in the opposite direction.) Mean excess returns were negative as often as they were positive for two weeks either side of a strike's beginning or ending. Thus it was unlikely an abnormal profit could be obtained and the profit would be eroded by transaction costs. Aside from the market reaction on the date the strike was announced, there were negative abnormal returns at two days and at 13 days prior to the strike. This indicated an efficient market reaction to the increasing probability of a strike. Neumann calculated that the market price of a company with market-price equity of $500 million 14 days before a strike would lose $4.6 million in market value after 14 days of strike length. It was particularly interesting to note that when a strike ended, there were not sufficient positive excess returns to compensate for the losses due to the strike period. This would support the contention that there are costs attached to a labor union which are differential from those of nonunion firms.

Ruback and Zimmerman (1984) tested the effect on a firm's stock price of first-time petitions to hold a union election and the subsequent certification of results by the NLRB on a firm's stock price. They tested the effect on stock price at the two events individually and as a combined effect. The results obtained showed that the abnormal returns in the petition month were -1.38 percent. Where the petition was followed by the union losing the election, the abnormal return in the petition month was -1.10 percent. This was interpreted as evidence that unions lower profits. There was not a statistically significant change in the returns at the certification date. Combining the effects of petition and certification dates into one combined measure, Ruback and Zimmerman found that for all 253 firms in the sample, the combined result was a net 1.86 percent loss to shareholders. Unions losing the election resulted in a 1.32 percent loss. Unions winning the election resulted in a 3.84 percent loss. These results were consistent with our expectations under efficient markets: the petition event itself is sufficient to generate abnormal returns.

Becker and Olson (1986) examined stock price changes in firms settling labor disputes with strikes and without strikes. The data for the study came from the Bureau of Labor Statistics' *Current Work Stoppages*. The strike study used a minimum strike size of 1,000 or more workers for the years 1962-1982. Daily return data were obtained from the CRSP tape. Compustat data were used to estimate the dollar cost to shareholders of a strike. These data were available for firms involved in 535 out of 699 total strikes in the sample. The sample was limited to firms listed on either the NYSE or AMEX exchanges and excluded any strike with a pre-event period which overlapped the event period of a different strike against the same company. The net sample contained 699 strikes, with a mean number of involved employees of 5,500. A separate sample of 96 observations of nonstriking settlements was taken from 1977-1980 data in *Current Contract Settlements*.

Becker and Olson used ordinary least squares (OLS) regressions in event study methodology. Their study used daily return data, as did the Neumann (1980) study. One difference between the two papers was that Neumann did not test firms having a labor dispute which was settled peacefully (e.g., without a strike). To test the differences, Becker and Olson estimated a market model for each firm to model expected returns without a strike for the period of 180 days before the strike to 80 days before the strike. Data for the period of 80 days prior to 31 days prior to the strike were used to calculate prediction error variance. The expected returns for the time frame beginning 30 days before the strike and ending 30 days after the strike ended were estimated and then deducted from actual returns to determine any excess returns.

The results showed different market reactions to strikes and peaceful settlements of labor disputes. For the strike sample for the full period of 1962-1982, the cumulative average return was -4.16 percent, which was significantly less than zero. For striking firms in 1977-1980, the cumulative average return was -1.53 percent. Both results were significantly less than that found in the sample of peaceful settlements. However for the same period in the nonstrike sample, the cumulative average return was +3.03 percent, not significantly different from zero. Thus a positive market reaction to peaceful settlements was seen. Total strike costs to shareholders were also estimated. After converting all years to 1980 dollars, the average strike was found to have cost $87 million in the Compustat sample of 535 strikes, or 3.69 percent of equity. There were wide ranges in this measure. In the air transport industry, 22 strikes cost an average of $91 million each and on average decreased stockholder equity by 14.74 percent. The other extreme occurred in the tire and rubber goods industry, where 27 strikes on average increased equity by 2.2 percent, or $24 million. The last result was evidence that the market anticipated strikes. For the 30 days preceding a strike deadline, the cumulative average return fell by a significant amount for those firms which would be struck. The returns did not change significantly in the nonstrike sample.

Bronars and Deere (1990) performed an event study, based on election data from Ruback and Zimmerman, of the stock price effects of union organization elections. The sample was Ruback and Zimmerman's representation election sample, modified to eliminate firms with multiple elections (simultaneous elections within the firm, but in different bargaining units), and to eliminate all union elections prior to 1965. The net sample was 198 elections held between 1965 and September 1980 in 105 different companies listed on the New York Stock Exchange, involving a minimum of 750 employees. The dependent variable was the percent excess return on equity during the event month (either petition or certification). Bronars and Deere found that successful union elections were anticipated as of the petition date. Petitions for elections that were successful lowered a firm's market value by two percent more than unsuccessful elections. Firms in industries which had higher unionization rates were related to significantly higher equity losses: "A 10 percentage point increase in an industry's average unionization rate implies an additional decline in equity value of .46 - .87 per cent." (28) Excess returns for the certification month were not significant, suggesting that the market impounded relevant information into the stock price in the petition month. Right-to-work laws had no effect on expected losses. Lastly, equity losses from unionization attempts were expected to increase by .2 per cent every year.

Huth and MacDonald (1990) conducted an event study of NYSE and AMEX listed firms to test for abnormal returns due to decertification petitions and elections. The net sample included 203 listed firms which had decertification elections in the period June 1977 through May 1987, involving more than 250 employees. Daily election data were obtained through Freedom of Information requests to regional NLRB offices. Daily return data were obtained from the CRSP tapes.

Multiple elections within firms were treated in the manner prescribed by Ruback and Zimmerman (1984). If the election outcomes were the same for overlapping decertification elections, the total set of overlapped elections was considered to be one event. The first petition date was considered the petition filing date and the last certification date became the election certification date. Those observations with differing election outcomes were excluded from the sample.

The event study examined abnormal returns to individual firms (which varied from the estimated market return) at two event dates: the petition filing date and the effective date the NLRB certified the results of the election. The period tested for each observation was 239 days prior to the event to estimate the market model, and 21 days around the event (ten days before and ten days after the event).

Results obtained indicated that the petition filing date failed to provide much new information. For all firms involved in a decertification election, the cumulative abnormal return on the petition filing date did not vary significantly from zero. There was a significant negative return nine days before the event. There was considerable new information from the election certification date, however. For those firms in which the decertification was successful (the union lost) the cumulative abnormal return was +0.653 on the day the election result was certified. For firms whose unions won the decertification vote, the CAR was -0.611. Both results were significant at the .01 level. This supported the idea of differential market reactions to the outcome of a decertification election and was consistent with other work which suggested that unions reduced the profitability of companies in the view of the market.

Kiss, Hexter, Curcio, and Williams (1990) conducted an event study of strikes and peaceful settlements both before and after the Professional Air Traffic Controllers' Organization (PATCO) strike in 1981. President Reagan fired the striking controllers, and this strike with its attendant federal intervention was used as an event which might have changed the cost of strikes to shareholders. This strike was seen as a signal that firm management could begin to replace striking workers with cheaper employees. The sample included strikes settled between January 1974 and December 1987; it also included a sample of settlements reached without a strike for the same period. The minimum size of labor dispute covered in this study had 1,000 employees covered by the collective bargaining agreement. Sample sizes were as follows:

	Pre-PATCO	Post-PATCO
Time period	7 1/2 years before August 1981	6 1/2 years after August 1981
Strikes	342 observations	123 observations (n=465)
Peaceful settlements	113 observations	87 observations (n=200)

Data specifications for the sample required daily return data on the 1987 CRSP tape and selected asset data for each firm on the 1988 Compustat tape for computing the degree of capital intensity. Strikes in the construction industry and in the public sector were excluded. Observations were excluded if the pre-event period of one strike overlapped the event period for another dispute (strike or peaceful settlement) in the same firm. The data on 1982-1987 strikes were obtained from *Current Wage Developments* published by the Bureau of Labor Statistics. Strike data for 1974-1981 were gathered from *Industrial Relations Facts Weekly*, also by the Bureau of Labor Statistics. Data for the peaceful settlement sample were listed in *Current Wage Developments*.

The methodology for this research was regression analysis in an event study design, in which mean abnormal returns and cumulative average returns were calculated for all observations. The four different samples described above were then compared to determine if their returns differed from each of the other three. The result determined whether strikes before PATCO had the same effect on stockholder wealth as those strikes after PATCO. The market model was estimated and regressed over a period of 230 days pre-event to 30 days pre-event. This yielded market model coefficients for each firm in the sample and based on these the expected returns were calculated. Actual returns for each firm were calculated as dividends plus stock appreciation divided by the original purchase price.

The results obtained indicated that there was a difference in the cost of strikes to shareholders, depending on whether the strike was before or after PATCO. While strikes in both periods were related to negative cumulative average returns, only those for the pre-PATCO strikes were significantly different from zero. For peaceful settlements, none of the CARs were significantly different from zero.

Pearce, Groff, and Wingender (1990) extended the work of Ruback and Zimmerman (discussed earlier). Their research tested stock price effects of union decertification elections for the period January 1963 through December 1986. A minimum size bargaining unit of 100 employees was required for inclusion in the sample. The gross sample amounted to 277 cases, with the final sample which was tested having 153 cases of decertification elections. This final sample was divided between firms which retained the union (78) and those which ousted the union (75). The test methodology was an event study using daily data to measure daily excess returns. The returns to an equally weighted CRSP market portfolio were regressed against the returns to each individual company's stock to model the firm's return generating process:

$$R_{it} = \alpha_i + B_i R_{mt} + e_{it}$$

where:

R_{it} = the observed (actual) daily return for an individual stock i on day t;

R_{mt} = CRSP equally weighted market index return for day t;

α_i = intercept slope;

B_i = slope coefficient; and

e_{it} = an error term.

The coefficients for the market model were estimated for each decertification case for a window of from 135 trading days prior to the filing date of the decertification petition to 16 trading days prior to the filing of the petition.

There were three events in decertification: petition filing date, election date, and the date the election results were announced (the certification date). For each case these three test periods were used. Each period was 15 days on either side of the event, for a 31 day test period. Abnormal returns were computed for each day of each test period. The abnormal return was the change between each firm's predicted return and the actual return observed. For the entire sample ($n = 153$), cumulative abnormal returns showed a steady increase over the three weeks prior to petition filing date. CARs totaled 1.28% over the three weeks, including the petition date. Abnormal returns were at the highest (and most significant) level on the petition day, at +0.4334.

The positive sign was interpreted as meaning that the market saw decertification as "good news." Other significant abnormal returns were observed five days prior to the petition date, and at six, seven, and ten days after the petition date. The test of the election date did not provide as many significant abnormal returns: abnormal returns were found seven and six days prior to the election date and at four days after. The certification date provided abnormal returns only at ten days post certification date.

For each event tested, only the petition date had overall significant stock price activity. The authors noted that "...the stock price response indicates that the stock market agents believe that the filing of a decertification petition is good news for the firm involved." (16) Investor gains made up through the petition date were completely lost in the first seven trading days post-event. This was interpreted as an indication that the market "...lacked confidence in the long term benefits to the firm from decertification." (16)

A partitioned sample for those companies where the union was retained (n=78) and those companies where the union was ousted (n=75) was tested. For the companies which kept the union, there was no significant response to the petition filing. The group which ousted the union had "large positive abnormal returns" which were described in the full sample results above. The research of Pearce et al. was significant because it was the first time that the effect of a decertification election on equity value had been demonstrated. This was also the first attempt to differentiate structural cost change from labor cost change. Structural costs were subject to change when the labor/management relation in a company changed. The partitioned sample tested (above) demonstrated that there existed a "prolonged and significant (stock) price response" when the union was retained as bargaining agent (21). This was interpreted as meaning that investors believed that not incurring structural change costs (going from union to non-union labor) was more important than any gains from eliminating the union.

Hirsch and Morgan (1994) calculated the systematic risk and rate of return to shareholders of union versus non-union firms. The sample was composed of 400 domestic manufacturing firms, for the period 1973-1987. The sample was an unbalanced panel with data for each firm coming from the Manufacturing Sector Master File, Compustat, and other sources. Union coverage for each firm was sourced from an earlier survey by the first author.

Shareholder risk and return were calculated from the market model,

$$R_{it} = a_i + b_i R_{mt} + e_{it}$$

where:

R_{it} = the rate of return for firm $_i$ in period $_t$, equal to dividends plus stock price increase (decrease) between last period $_{t-1}$ and the current period $_t$, all divided by the price paid in period $_{t-1}$;

R_{mt} = market rate of return for the NYSE Composite Index;

a_i = intercept slope;

b_i = firm-specific beta; and

e_{it} = an error term.

Beta for each firm was calculated for each year 1973 through 1987. Subsequently, regression analysis was performed with firm beta as the dependent variable. The results obtained regarding shareholder risk suggested that there was lower shareholder risk in union companies than nonunion companies through 1981, but this difference had largely disappeared during the 1980s. With respect to returns, Hirsch and Morgan found nonunion companies had higher returns than union companies for six consecutive years, 1977-1982. For this six-year period, the results indicated a 24 percent decrease in market value for the unionized firms (with a mean 40 percent union coverage) compared to nonunion firms of similar risk belonging to the same industry group. This disparity reversed from 1983-1987, with union firms providing higher returns to investors than nonunion firms. Overall for the 15 year period there were no differences in returns between the two groups.

Overall, research into union effects on stock prices has been focused on elections or strikes, using event study methodology; or union coverage. The following summarizes results from that research.

Elections:

First-time petitions for elections and the elections, generally reduced the market value of the firm's stock. The degree of loss was sensitive to the specific union seeking representation rights (Ruback and Zimmerman, 1984).

There was a cumulative abnormal return which was positive if the union lost a representation election and negative if the union won a representation election. The magnitude of the CAR was almost identical (Huth and MacDonald, 1990).

Firms which decertified their unions experienced large positive returns at the petition date; firms which kept their unions had no significant response at the petition date. The market had different reactions to decertifications, and these were inconsistent with the longer-term market response in favor of firms which retained their unions. This supported the need for a longer-term study of firm performance of the differences between representation and decertification elections (Pearce, Groff, and Wingender, 1990).

Successful union elections were anticipated as of the petition date. Petitions for elections that were successful lowered a firm's market value by two percent more than unsuccessful elections. Higher unionization rates in a firm's industry were related to significantly higher equity losses. Excess returns for the certification month were not significant (Bronars and Deere, 1990).

Strikes:

Strikes were related to overall negative abnormal returns. Struck firms yielded negative returns when struck and positive returns on settlement, the net effect of which was negative. Therefore labor costs to shareholders were differential between union and nonunion firms, because of potential strike losses in unionized firms (Neumann, 1980).

Similar to Neumann, Becker and Olson found that strikes reduced the equity value of a firm. Extending Neumann's work, a sample of peaceful settlements (by negotiation) to labor disputes exhibited a positive market reaction, significantly different from the CAR of the struck firms (Becker and Olson, 1986).

Since the government's attitude about enforcing labor rights to strike has been demonstrated via PATCO, only strikes prior to the PATCO strike had significant costs to shareholders (Kiss, Hexter, Curcio and Williams, 1990).

Strikes at large firms were associated with differing levels of cumulative average residuals, depending on the length of the strike. Strikes of ten days or less were related to below-market CARs before, during, and after a strike. The CAR indicated a weak firm before and after the strike. Middle-length strikes (11 to 29 days) were associated with market level CARs which rose post-strike, indicative of shareholders' satisfaction with the end of the strike. Long strikes were found related to high CARS pre-strike, which dropped following settlement. These signaled firms with excess profits available for union capture, in which shareholders were dissatisfied with the outcome. Since the outcome of the strike in monetary terms was not examined, this explanation of the underlying reason for the behavior of the residuals was open (Greer, Martin, and Reusser, 1980).

Union coverage:

Nonunion companies had higher returns than union companies for 1977-1982; during this period, organized companies experienced a 24 percent decrease in market value. For the following years 1983-1987, union firms provided higher returns to investors than nonunion firms. For the 15 year test period overall, there were no differences in returns between the two groups (Hirsch and Morgan, 1994).

COMPENSATION

Freeman and Medoff (1981) identified union effects on wages in manufacturing industries. They found a direct relationship between increased levels of the degree to which a labor force was organized (belongs to a union) and wage levels. The union wage effect in a manufacturing industry that was 80 percent organized was about nine percent higher than in an industry that was 20 percent organized. Firm size, measured in shipment value, was also associated with wage levels in a positive and significant manner. While this study did not address pension expenses, it is significant for the reason that it provides support for part of the present research methodology. The research design in Chapter III is based on a change in the level of union organization (indicated by an election). Additionally, Freeman and Medoff support the ideas that as unions influence wage levels, pensions (as a fringe benefit related to wages) may also be influenced by unions. This was one of the findings in the next study.

Freeman (1981) in a large-scale study of union effects on fringe benefits found that unionism was related to significant increases in the monetary amounts spent for pensions, as well as the percentage of wages allotted to pensions. Freeman found that the percentage of union hourly compensation allotted to pensions in manufacturing establishments was twice as high as in nonunion manufacturing. For all private nonfarm establishments, the union percentage was three times higher (490):

Freeman noted that unionism had two separate effects on compensation: that of "...unions raising the total level of compensation..." and that of "...unions possibly altering the fringe share of a given compensation package..."(490).

Belman and Voos (1993) tested two industries to determine whether use of mixed-industry datasets obscured relationships between the extent of union membership in an industry and union wages. The aerospace industry represented a national market, and supermarkets represented a local market industry. Data were obtained from the *Current Population Survey* for 1987 and 1989, published by the Bureau of Labor Statistics. There were 4,389 observations for supermarkets and 2,134 observations for aerospace. Results indicated that for the industry with a local market (supermarkets), individuals' wages would rise approximately 2.3 percent when union coverage of supermarkets increased ten percentage points. While union coverage was related to local markets, the reverse was true for national markets. Union coverage was not a significant factor for the national market aerospace industry. This provided support for the notion that contracts bargained on a national basis, as happens in the aerospace industry, were not influenced by the extent of local-level union membership.

PROFITABILITY

Clark (1984) tested the effects of the presence of a union on a business unit's rate of return on investment, rate of sales growth, and labor productivity. The unionization variable was the employers' estimates of what percentage of their employees were unionized. Clark found that unionized firms earned substantially lower returns than their nonunion competition.

Tests of return on investment (ROI) and return on sales (ROS) were found in Clark (1984). Clark used the PIMS dataset (composed of 902 "business units" (divisions of firms) engaged in specific four-digit industries) to examine how unionization affected profitability. The time period tested was 1970-1980. Each year that a firm appeared in the sample (firm-year) was treated as a separate observation. A total of 4,681 observations (five per firm on average) were included in the sample. Clark used regression analysis to make point estimates of the union effects on variables. The study was cross-sectional in nature, but the PIMS dataset was a nonrandom sample mainly composed of U.S. manufacturing companies. Profitability was defined as "rate of return on capital (ROI): net income (pretax) divided by total capital invested in the business." (903) Union data were obtained with a questionnaire which asked "of all the employees in this business, what percentage are unionized?" (906) Clark largely used a dichotomous variable for union or nonunion status.

Clark found "...a sizeable negative effect of unionization on profits..." (911) for both ROI and ROS. He reported a 12 percent decline in ROI for firms which were unionized, and when further controls for labor markets and market structure were included, ROI decreased 19 percent from the sample mean. Testing ROS, Clark found an 18 percent lower return on sales for unionized companies compared to nonunion firms.

Clark used two alternative measures of unionization and tested them independently. The results listed above were obtained using a dichotomous variable, with a zero representing a nonunion firm and a one representing any level of unionization. For the alternative, Clark used the percentage of employees unionized (as reported on his questionnaire) and placed these observations into three categories: unionization below 30 percent, from 30 to 60 percent, and more than 60 percent organized. No significant differences were found between the results of this test and the test using the dichotomous variable.

Salinger (1984) tested union effects on profits two ways, comparing Tobin's q ratio to accounting rate of return (ROI) as the dependent variable. (q was the ratio of the market value of a firm to the replacement value of its physical assets.) Tobin's q was a useful alternative to ROI as a profit measure, because it measured long-term monopoly power. Risk adjustment was incorporated through the use of market values. Salinger claimed that the q ratio was more accurately measured than profit rates (Salinger, 160). The author found that when concentration and barriers to entry were present, there was an opportunity for monopoly rents. Unions captured 77 percent of these monopoly rents. The union's members were the primary beneficiaries through receipt of increased wages.

Karier (1985) tested a cross-section of manufacturing industries for a "union effect" which would vary depending on the industry's concentration level. Concentrated industries were found to generate higher profits, and the higher the percentage of workers unionized in these industries, the lower the amount of realized monopoly profits the firms retained (e.g., the union captured 68 percent of the total monopoly profits).

Connolly, Hirsch, and Hirschey (1986) used a market value measure of profitability, relative excess valuation, to measure union effects on profits. Union density was defined at the industry level, not at firm level. The dependent variable was highly similar to Tobin's q ratio, as used in Salinger (1984). Relative excess valuation (EV/S) was a market value of profit which was divided by sales. The formula was:

$$EV/S = [MV(F) - BV(T)] / S,$$

where:

$BV(T)$ = book value of tangible assets;

S = sales; and

$MV(F)$ = market value of firm, computed as the total of the market value of tangible assets plus intangible assets.

EV/S and q were closely related; in this test the correlation between EV/S and q equalled 0.94. The results of OLS regressions (n = 367) for an overall union effect on profits was negative, at -0.087. (The partial derivative of relative excess valuation with respect to unionization was -0.087) This was interpreted to mean that a firm in an industry that was 50 percent unionized "would have an EV/S approximately (2.6%) lower than an otherwise similar firm" that was 20 percent unionized. (575)

Voos and Mishel (1986b) tested the supermarket industry to identify a relationship between the extent of a union's ability to reduce profits and monopoly conditions in the firm's marketplace. The degree of concentration (lack of competition) was the measure for monopoly conditions. The union variable was dichotomous. The researchers found that in the supermarket industry, unions reduced profits in concentrated markets by 65.8 percent. In competitive markets, unions reduced profits by 13.2 percent.

Voos and Mishel (1986a) used price-cost margin (PCM) as the measure of profitability. This was defined as

PCM = $\dfrac{\text{(value of shipments - materials cost - payroll)}}{\text{value of shipments}}$.

Data were gathered from industry databases, specifically the Annual Survey of Manufactures and the 1972 Census of Manufactures. Data were generated for 139 three-digit manufacturing industries. Voos and Mishel found that, using price-cost margin as the dependent regression variable, "...a fully unionized industry has a 22.6% lower PCM than an industry with no unionization." (118)

Becker and Olson (1992) examined unionization effects on large manufacturing firm profits. Two regression-based estimation models were used, with one reflecting market valuation and the second reflecting accounting values. The excess value model determined the difference between the market's valuation of a firm's assets and their cost. The price-cost margin model was based on accounting data, and was defined as gross profits before depreciation, divided by sales.

The sample included 297 large manufacturing firms with primary SIC codes of 20-39. All firms had filed the 1977 Annual Return/Report of Employee Benefit Plan (Form 5500). This included a union code, indicating whether the plan was negotiated between an employer and a union. The firm unionization percentage was calculated as the ratio of all union pension plan enrollments for a given firm, divided by total firm pension plan enrollment. Financial data for individual firms came from Compustat.

Becker and Olson found that complete unionization was not particularly important in generating significant differences in both models' estimates of profitability. The difference in the Price-Cost Margin model was three-fourths explained by the first ten percent of unionization in a firm. In the Excess Value model, virtually all of the difference was explained by the first ten percent unionization. Calculating the dollar value of the union effect on profits, Becker and Olson estimated that for their sample of large firms (all in the Fortune 1,000) "...that the effect of a 1 percent increase in unionization alters Excess Value entirely through its effect on the market value of the firm." (412) They further estimated that using a 1977 average weekly manufacturing salary of $228, the union effect was equal to a premium per worker of $1,147 after corporate tax of 50 percent, or $2,294 in actual compensation (412).

RESEARCH AND DEVELOPMENT

Several studies have tested for a linkage between unionization and expenditures for research and development. Connolly, Hirsch, and Hirschey (1986) tested the effects of a labor union's presence on a firm's intangible capital expenditures (such as advertising or research and development expenditures). In particular, the firm's R&D spending was tested in the study. Union density was defined at the industry level, not the firm level. For each firm's three-digit SIC code industry, union density was the proportion of eligible workers who were union members. Their study found that firms in highly unionized environments invested less in research and development. This type of intangible investment was found to add less to the market value of firms in more unionized industries.

Pakes (1985), in a study not addressing unionism, examined stock market reactions to R&D spending and patents obtained. He found that only recent or current environmental changes (those preceding by three years or less a change in R&D spending) led to the firm's changing its R&D spending. Pakes also found that patents were applied for fairly quickly after the underlying R&D expenditures were incurred: "About 50 percent of these patents will be applied for in the same year as the R&D expenditures are incurred, while 70 percent will be applied for within three years." (404)

Allen's study (1988) tested two different measures of R&D to determine union effects. For R&D which was originated in an industry, "The ratio of research and development originating to output (produced) is 12 percentage points less in an industry where all production workers belong to a union than in an industry where none do." (105) A second measure was an industry's use of R&D developed elsewhere. Allen found that the ratio of R&D used to output produced "...is 17 percentage points lower in unionized industries than in nonunionized industries." (105)

Hirsch (1992) examined 706 manufacturing firms to estimate the effects of union coverage on companies' investment in physical capital and in R&D. The period tested was 1972-1980. The sample included all domestic publicly traded manufacturing doing business in 1976, for which Compustat data were available for 1976-1978. The measure of union coverage was the percentage of each company's total North American workforce which was covered by collective bargaining agreements in 1977. During 1977, average union coverage was 33 percent (102). The sample was partitioned for nonunion firms, with zero union employees; below 30 percent union coverage was termed low coverage; over 30 percent but below 60 percent coverage was identified as medium coverage; and 60 percent or more union coverage was considered high coverage. The results obtained for companies' investment in research and development indicated that investment in R&D at unionized companies was 25 percent lower in low union coverage companies, compared to similar firms which were nonunion. Medium coverage firms invested 27 percent less than their nonunion peers. High coverage firms spent 35 percent less than similar firms which were nonunion. This measured direct effects; total direct and indirect effects were two percent higher for medium and high coverage firms. Union effects on investment in physical capital were found to be 15 percent less for low coverage firms. Medium coverage firms spent 23 percent less than their peers, and high coverage firms spent 17 percent less than similar nonunion firms.

The papers discussed above supported the concept of a union effect on firm- or industry-level performance measures. Much of the testing was done in manufacturing and in many cases unionization of these firms occurred in the 1940s and 1950s (Clark 1984). Presumably because of this there were no pre-unionization/post-unionization studies available. The evidence presented offered a picture of the potential distinctions among firms based on unionization.

RELEVANCE TO CURRENT STUDY

The literature reviewed above provided a basis for expectations of the empirical testing in the current study. Testing for changes in productivity was expected to result in at least a trend for productivity to have increased faster in companies where the union had lost a decertification election. In firms where the union had won a representation election, it was expected that these firms would have exhibited a lower rate of positive change than the firms in the related control groups. It was anticipated that profitability testing would have resulted in decreased return on investment if the union had won a representation election. Return on investment should have increased subsequent to a union loss of a decertification election. Research and development expenditures were expected to increase in firms which decertified their unions. Conversely R&D spending was expected to fall subsequent to a union winning a representation election. Pension and retirement expenses were expected to have increased in cases where the union won a representation election and to have decreased in cases where the union lost a decertification election. The specifications of these tests are found in Chapter III.

CHAPTER SUMMARY

This chapter examined literature related to accounting disclosure of information, and literature with respect to union effects on companies' financial performance. The disclosure literature supported the argument that unions were part of a firm's economic environment, and were differential among firms. The previous research in the disclosure area also supported disclosure of data on pensions, research and development, and labor contracts. These were among the variables in the current study.

The union effects literature was also reviewed. This body of research provided certain financial variables which were identified as being influenced by unionism. Among these variables were productivity, stock prices, compensation, profitability, and research and development.

Exhibit A presents a summary of the literature review. The next chapter presents the research methodology for the current study.

EXHIBIT A

SUMMARY OF THE LITERATURE REVIEW

Study and Date	Sample Date	Sample Size	Conclusions
Singhvi and Desai - 1971	1965	155 industrial firms	Rate of return and earnings margin were positively related to extent of disclosure
Buzby - 1974	1971	44 small and medium size firms	Items deemed important in annual statements included pension plan data research and development expenditures
Chandra - 1974	1974	498 professionals (Certified Public Accountants and Chartered Financial Analysts	R&D spending and productivity data were valued differently by analysts and users of financial statements
Patillo - 1976	1976	684 financial professionals and academics	Perceptions of materiality by readers of statements were influenced by political and economic characteristics
Brown and Medoff - 1978	1972	341 state-by-two digit SIC industries	Unionized establishments were 24% more productive; higher wage costs offset this gain
Clark - 1980	1953-1976	Six cement plants that from nonunion to union	Unionization resulted in a 6-8% increase in productivity and 12 - 18% wage increase

EXHIBIT A

SUMMARY OF THE LITERATURE REVIEW

Study and Date	Sample Date	Sample Size	Conclusions
Greer, Martin and Reusser 1980	1951-1976	91 strikes in firms	Cumulative average residuals differed by length of strike in days
Neumann - 1980	1967-1975	340 firms struck	Negative excess returns due to strikes were not reversed when strike ended; excess returns were not large enough to surpass trading costs
Freeman - 1981	1967-1972	10,088 establishments	Pension expenses were 2 to 3 times higher for union firms than nonunion firms
Freeman and Medoff - 1981	1968-1975	Current population	Wages rise with percent organized. Firms 80% organized have 9% higher wages than a firm 20% organized
Link - 1981	1973-1978	51 firms in seven industries	Productivity growth was growth was 2.5% slower if unionized
Link - 1982	1975-1979	97 firms in three industries	Productivity growth was 9.2% to 10.3% slower if unionized

EXHIBIT A

SUMMARY OF THE LITERATURE REVIEW

Study and Date	Sample Date	Sample Size	Conclusions
Clark - 1984	1970-1980	902 product-line businesses	Union firms are 1% more productive; union firms with under 10% market share are 40% less profitable. ROI is 12 to 19% less for unionized firms; ROS is 18% lower for unionized firms
Hirsch and Link 1984	1957-1973	19 two-digit SIC industries	Productivity growth 3.6 to 4.4% slower if unionized
Ruback and Zimmerman 1984	1962-1980	253 union elect-ions involving over 750 employ-ees of NYSE-listed firms	First-time petitions reduced market value of stock 1.38%. Union election wins cost 3.84% of equity market value
Salinger - 1984	1979	175 mfg. firms	Unions captured 77% monopoly profits
Karier - 1985	1972	341 firms in 20 two-digit SIC industries	Unions captured 68% of of monopoly profits
Pakes - 1985	1968-1975	120 firms which filed patent applications	Changes in R&D expendi-tures were almost entirely determined by events within three previous years

EXHIBIT A

SUMMARY OF THE LITERATURE REVIEW

Study and Date	Sample Date	Sample Size	Conclusions
Becker and Olson - 1986	1962-1982	699 strikes in 535 firms	Average strike costs 3.69% of equity; peaceful settlement of a labor dispute generated +3.03% cumulative average return; a strike resulted in a -4.16% cumulative average return
Connolly, Hirsch and Hirschey - 1986	1977	367 firms in Fortune 500	R&D spending decreased as unionization increased wages increased 12-18%
Voos and Mishel - 1986a	1970-1974	71 firms in supermarket industry	Unions reduced profits by 13%
Voos and Mishel - 1986b	1967	139 3-digit manufacturing industries	Price-cost margin 23% lower in completely unionized firms, compared to nonunion firms
Allen - 1988	1972-1983	74 3- and 4-digit SIC industries for which output indexes are published	Productivity increased with union level, but was statistically insignificant

EXHIBIT A

SUMMARY OF THE LITERATURE REVIEW

Study and Date	Sample Date	Sample Size	Conclusions
Bronars and Deere - 1990	1965-1980	198 representation elections in 105 NYSE-listed firms	Petitions for successful elections lower market value 2% more than unsuccessful elections; higher industry unionization rate was related to higher equity loss
Huth and MacDonald 1990	1977-1987	203 firms	Cumulative abnormal return was +0.653 on date of certification of union loss of a decertification election; for union winning, the CAR was -0.611
Kiss, Hexter, Curcio, and Williams - 1990	1974-1987	465 strikes and 200 peaceful settlements	Only pre-PATCO strikes were significant to significant to shareholders
Pearce, Groff, and Wingender 1990	1963-1986	153 decertification elections	Firms decertifying unions had large positive returns at petition date; firms retaining unions had no significant response at petition date

EXHIBIT A

SUMMARY OF THE LITERATURE REVIEW

Study and Date	Sample Date	Sample Size	Conclusions
Becker and Olson - 1992	1977	297 manufac-turing firms	The first 10% of unioni-zation explained 75% of the difference in Price-Cost Margin and virtually all the difference in Excess Value; the union premium per worker was $2,294 annually
Hirsch - 1992	1972-1980	706 manufac-turing firms	R&D investment in firms with unionization <30% was 25% less than non-union firms; <60% union-ization was 27% less; and >60% unionization was 35% less. Similar results obtained for investments in physical capital
Mitchell and Stone - 1992	1986	96 sawmills	Unionized sawmills were 12 to 26% less productive than nonunion mills
Belman and Voos - 1993	1987, 1989	4,389 individ-uals in super-market industry and 2,134 indiv-iduals in aero-space industry	Wages were related to union density for local market industry; 10 percentage points rise in union membership would generate a 2.3% rise in wages. Local area union density was not significant in wage estimation for a national market industry

EXHIBIT A

SUMMARY OF THE LITERATURE REVIEW

Study and Date	Sample Date	Sample Size	Conclusions
Hirsch and Morgan - 1994	1973-1987	400 manufacturing firms	Unionized firms had lower shareholder risk through 1981; Unionized firms had lower returns to shareholders 1977-1982, equal to a 24% decrease in market value with mean union coverage of 40%. Union firms generated higher returns 1983-1987. No difference over long-term in returns

III

Research Questions And Methodology

STATEMENT OF THE PROBLEM

From the preceding discussion it is clear that there exist "union effects" which are reflected in a firm's financial statements. Since all firms are not equal with respect to unionization of their employees, union effects are differential among firms. As the previous chapter indicated, only recently has there been any recognition of the effect of labor unions on firms and a body of research dealing directly with the firm-union link is small.

There is a related issue which previous research has not addressed: What happens to the unionized firm whose union "disappears" by being voted out of office as the bargaining agent? Based upon the current literature, it is reasonable to consider whether these union effects will reverse or at least partly mitigate after union decertification. This provides a basis for questioning whether accounting disclosure should include unionism.

This study differs from existing research in several ways. First, the group of firms from which data were drawn has not been tested previously for any financial or economic effects related to unionism.

Second, the results of decertification elections in firms have not been investigated from the viewpoint of testing for differences in firm performance. The labor-management relation begins with a union winning a representation election and terminates when employees decertify their union. While first-time unionism and existing unionism have been investigated, no research has examined the end of the relationship, which occurs with decertification of the union.

Third, no research has been identified which considered both representation and decertification elections for the same time periods and industries. Representation elections are held when 30 percent of a firm's work force signs cards to hold the election. This information is communicated to the National Labor Relations Board (NLRB), which supervises the election process. The Board sets an election date and the election is held. If a majority of those employees eligible to vote do cast votes for the union as their agent for collective bargaining, the union wins and is certified by the Board as the bargaining unit's agent. If the union loses the representation election, then there is not a collective bargaining agent for the employees; in effect the employees speak for themselves to the employer.

In the event that employees become dissatisfied with an incumbent union, union members have the right to elect not to be represented any longer by their union. This is done through a decertification election. If a majority of the employees vote to decertify the union, the union loses its authority to represent the employees in that bargaining unit at that employer.

Fourth, no prior study recognized that union effects are in fact a disclosure issue. The present study integrated union effects into the larger issue of accounting disclosure through an empirical test. The test used data from a large population of publicly traded firms to determine if four variables used to measure selected union effects were sufficiently influenced by isolated union elections, compared to similar firms with no elections, to suggest that the union election was an event which should be disclosed in the firm's financial statements.

This study examined what happened to four specific measures of operating performance when a company's employees held a decertification or representation election for a labor union. The items tested were profitability, research and development expenditures, pension and retirement expenses, and productivity. As reported in the previous chapter, these four outcome measures represented direct measures of union influence on firms or industries which have been empirically tested and found to have significant relationships. Other measures of union influence were tested in these previous papers, but were insignificant. In the literature, stock market prices were considered a subset of the profitability tests (Voos and Mishel, 1986a, 107) along with return on investment, return on sales, and price-cost margin. The research in this book observed changes between pre-event measures and equivalent post-event measures, as described later. It was not possible to anticipate the direction of the change in any given variable. Thus, the investigation focused on whether there was a change in profitability, research and development expenditures, pension and retirement expenses, and productivity.

IMPORTANCE OF THE TOPIC

There have been studies performed which found a need for increased disclosures, including items related to or influenced by labor unions. Other studies have approached the topic from another direction, and tested for union effects on certain variables. These empirical studies have found that unions are associated with demonstrable and significant effects on stock prices, profitability, productivity, and monopoly profits. None of these changes which are associated with labor unions are required to be disclosed under the current accounting and reporting requirements. Disclosure about a firm's relationship with labor unions is largely a matter of management discretion. None of the prior studies has used the union election as an event to test empirically whether a need exists for increased disclosure. None of these are captured under the current accounting and reporting requirements.

This current research represents the first attempt to use an empirical test of firm level financial data and union election data to answer questions about the adequacy of existing disclosure requirements. If significant results regarding the effect of labor union elections on financial variables were found, the evidence would indicate the extent of changes in firm performance due to increases or decreases (or potential increases or decreases) in employees' union membership. Decertification elections are an increasing proportion of total union elections, with representation elections making up the balance (National Labor Relations Board Annual Report, Table 17, various years). Thus, the issue of disclosure of union effects seems likely to grow in importance.

This research should be of interest to financial accounting theorists, financial analysts, and management. Because the labor union status of a firm's employees was not (and is not currently) a required disclosure item, changes in the level of unionization within a firm are not part of the data used for decision making. Evidence of changes in firms' profitability, productivity, R&D spending, and pension expenses linked to decreases or increases in union membership would represent new information to all of the groups noted above. Knowledge of whether union effects were reversible would facilitate forecasts of future results. Clearer evidence of the costs and benefits of unionization would provide additional useful information and explanatory power to complement the variable set now used. The useful information would provide a measure of the robustness of results already obtained (and perhaps clarify some of the conflicting results) and it would extend knowledge of the process driving the generation of security returns by specifying the contribution of certain non-accounting data. This research contributed a study of many firms, using individual company-specific data rather than industry-level data to a research area where such studies are scarce. Many prior studies used industry-level measures of unionism.

RESEARCH QUESTIONS

The purpose of this study was to examine the financial differences that union decertification or representation elections may cause in publicly traded companies to determine whether union data should be disclosed in the financial statements. In order to answer this, it was necessary to ask whether union elections had any significant effect on four variables. The variables tested were research and development expenditures per employee, pension and retirement expenditures per employee, profitability, and productivity. These variables were the basis for the four principal research questions discussed below. Following the presentation of the research questions a discussion of the testing design is given. The statistical hypotheses are developed after the testing design.

The four research questions related to performance of the firm which had experienced a union election with respect to specific measures for R&D expenditures, pension benefits, profitability, and productivity.

Research Question 1

Were research and development expenditures on a per-employee basis significantly different between firms which have experienced a union election and those which have not?

Research Question 2

Were pension and retirement expenses per employee significantly different between firms which have experienced a union election and those which have not?

Research Question 3

Was profitability significantly different between firms which have experienced a union election and those which have not?

Research Question 4

Was productivity, measured on the basis of sales per employee, significantly different between firms which have experienced a union election and those which have not?

The next section discusses the testing design used to make the four research questions operational. Following that, the formal statements of hypotheses are presented.

TESTING DESIGN

To answer the research questions it was necessary to measure the performance of firms in different industries which had experienced union elections in different years of the test period.

It was acknowledged that any firm's performance could improve or degrade over time, and that such a change might or might not have been related to any change in unionism. Individual firm performance might have changed because its industry was changing, or because of changes in the general economy, or because of other factors. While a firm with a union election might have experienced a change in any of the four variables tested, without some similar firm(s) to compare results against, it would not be possible to claim the change (positive or negative) was due to the change in unionism.

To provide a basis for comparison, unique control groups were constructed for each observation. Each control group was a composite of one or more firms in the same primary industry but which had not had a union election during the entire test period. These control groups represented firms in the same industry with no increases or decreases in unionism for each observation to be compared against.

Each of the four variables (R&D per employee, pension and retirement expenditures per employee, sales per employee, and return on investment) were measured before and after a selected union election. The changes between the pre-election and post-election measures occurring in each variable were computed for each observation. The same was done for each firm in each control group (which represented the industry change). Changes in the firms with union elections were then compared with the industry control group for each of these firms. This was accomplished by finding the difference between the company change and the industry change over the same period. The measurements necessary to do this were:

Company change = After - Before,
Industry change = Average effect for a given variable for the
            period for others in the industry with no election, and
Difference = Company change - Industry change.

(note that the industry change was operationally used as the control group change).

Campbell and Stanley (1966, 43) termed this type of design an equivalent time samples design. This was considered a more powerful univariate test than t-tests of the differences between means of independently selected samples (Neely and Rochester 1987, 117). The null and alternate hypotheses for such a test were:

Ho: Company change - industry change = 0;
Ha: Company change - industry change ≠ 0.

This was the form of the univariate test for each hypothesis discussed below.

HYPOTHESES

This section presents the hypotheses used to make the research questions operational. First the research question to be answered is presented; variable definitions are explained; then the statistical hypotheses are discussed.

Hypothesis 1

The first research question was:

Were research and development expenditures on a per-employee basis significantly different between firms which have experienced a union election and those which have not?

Research and development (R&D) was defined as annual R&D expense divided by the average number of employees for the year. Data definitions appear in Appendix A. R&D was available annually, due to correcting adjustments normally being made to the accounts only at year-end for audit and financial statement purposes. The average employee count was constructed by adding the current year's employee count to the prior year's count and dividing in half.

To test this hypothesis, the pre-event date was the end of the year preceding the union election and the post-event date was the end of the year following the year of the union election. Statistically, the null and alternative hypotheses tested were:

$$Ho^1: DiffR\&D_t - DiffR\&D_c = 0.$$
$$Ha^1: DiffR\&D_t - DiffR\&D_c \neq 0.$$

where:

DiffR&D was equal to the mean of the post-election measure for annual research and development expenditures on a per-employee basis minus the pre-election measure for annual research and development expenditures on a per-employee basis. $_t$ denoted test observations. $_c$ denoted control group observations.

This hypothesis was tested for differences between firms which had elections and those which did not. The observations were also partitioned by election type and election outcome. The four possible cases were: representation elections won by unions, representation elections lost by unions, decertification elections won by unions, and decertification elections lost by unions. Each observation was compared to its unique control group. The hypothesis was also tested at two years post-election to determine whether changes in the variable continued, abated, or increased as more time passed since the election. This second year of testing was performed for the remaining hypotheses also.

Hypothesis 2

The second research question was:

Were per-employee pension and retirement expenses significantly different between firms which have experienced a union election and those which have not?

The variable of interest for this hypothesis was defined as annual pension and retirement expenses divided by average employee count.

Pensions and retirement benefits represent deferred compensation traded off against current income. Pensions are a mandatory bargaining item (Fossum 1982, 171-172) meaning that if pensions (or any of numerous other possible benefits) are offered by an employer, they must be bargained during contract negotiations. Unionism would appear to increase both the absolute and relative amounts of compensation given to pensions. Therefore it was reasonable to inquire what might happen to pension expense when unionism changes or faces the prospect of change. The pre-event date was the end of the year prior to the election. The post-event date was the end of the year following the year of election.

The null and alternative forms of the hypothesis tested were:

$$Ho^2: DiffPEN_t - DiffPEN_c = 0;$$
$$Ha^2: DiffPEN_t - DiffPEN_c \neq 0.$$

where:

DiffPEN was equal to the mean of the post-election measure for annual pension and retirement expenses on a per-employee basis minus the pre-election measure for annual pension and retirement expenses on a per-employee basis. Test observations were denoted by $_t$ and $_c$ indicated control group observations.

As for hypothesis 1, this hypothesis was tested for each of the four election outcome groups compared to the control group.

Hypothesis 3

The third research question was:

Was profitability significantly different between firms which have experienced a union election and those which have not?

To test this question, return on investment (ROI) was calculated for the year preceding the union election, the year following the union election, and for the second year following the union election. The test of this hypothesis followed the format described above for the first two hypotheses. Return on investment was defined as net income divided by total assets, on an annual basis. The null and alternative statistical hypotheses tested were:

$$\text{Ho}^3\text{: DiffROI}_t - \text{DiffROI}_c = 0;$$
$$\text{Ha}^3\text{: DiffROI}_t - \text{DiffROI}_c \neq 0.$$

where:

DiffROI was equal to the mean of the post-election measure for return on investment minus the pre-election measure for return on investment. Test observations were denoted by $_t$ and $_c$ indicated control group observations.

Hypothesis 4

The fourth research question was:

Was productivity, measured on the basis of sales per employee, significantly different between firms which have experienced a union election and those which have not?

To test this hypothesis, the pre-event date was the end of the year prior to the year in which the election occurred and the post-event date was the end of the year following the election. The second year after the election was also tested.

Productivity was defined as annual net sales divided by average employee count.   To test this question, the null and alternative hypotheses were:

$$Ho^4: DiffSLS_t - DiffSLS_c = 0;$$
$$Ha^4: DiffSLS_t - DiffSLS_c \neq 0.$$

where:

DiffSLS was equal to the mean of the post-election measure for annual sales per employee minus the pre-election measure for annual sales per employee.   Test observations were denoted by $_t$ and $_c$ indicated group observations.

The next section, Research Methodology, presents support for the methodology used to test these hypotheses.

RESEARCH METHODOLOGY

The phenomena of representation and decertification elections are historical events driven by the voting results of union members within individual firms. The event of interest was not subject to manipulation by the researcher, nor was it possible to randomly assign firms to treatment and control groups. To test this case, an ex post facto, quasi-experimental design was required. Kerlinger (1986, 348) states:

> "Nonexperimental research is systematic empirical inquiry in which the scientist does not have direct control of independent variables because their manifestations have already occurred or because they are inherently not manipulable.   Inferences about relations among variables are made, without direct intervention, from concomitant variation of independent and dependent variables."

The purpose of this study was to examine the financial differences that union decertification or representation votes may cause in publicly traded companies in order to assess the adequacy of current disclosure requirements. The principal research questions were whether the performance of firms with labor elections differed from the performance of firms without labor elections. As a frame of reference, the change in a firm's financial data was compared to changes over the same time period for similar firms which did not experience a union election. The methodology for this study identified the group of domestic publicly traded firms in which labor elections (either decertification or representation) have been held during the period 1978 through 1989 whose financial statement data were available through Compustat. The various subgroups which were identified within this large group are discussed in the next section.

THE ELECTION AND CONTROL GROUPS

This study used union elections in publicly traded companies as observations. The election year became the reference point for pretest-posttest measurements of financial variables. Union elections were viewed as a signal for labor unrest which in a given company had reached a sufficiently high level that an election could be called. Since a union election may have increased unionism in a company (if the union wins a representation election) or decreased it (if the union lost a decertification election), the election indicated employee desire for a change in unionism in that company. It was possible that a company's labor force was dissatisfied, but that this dissatisfaction did not result in an election. Barring an election, there was no way of measuring this type of dissatisfaction. Consequently, this study did not extend to firms which had not experienced an election.

Since 1977, when the NLRB added firm name to the labor record, there have been about 70,624 total (representation and decertification) labor elections. Of these, 9,497 have been decertification elections, and the balance were representation elections. Matching these names against the Standard and Poor's Directory yielded a group of publicly traded companies for which a control group could be composed.

Two criteria for inclusion in the test dataset were established. First, the firm must have been publicly traded and carried as an observation on the annual Standard and Poor's Compustat Annual tapes. This requirement ensured that data were treated consistently.

Second, the beginning date for a firm to enter the dataset was 1978. The first year the National Labor Relations Board (NLRB) included the firm name in the election records was 1977; beginning with 1978 allowed use of 1977 data for pre-event measurements.

Because of a requirement that test observations not have had an election within two years of the election date being tested (to isolate the election observation in question), the group of observations which met the criteria was 181 observations for tests of one year after the election and 129 observations for two years after the election. These are presented in Appendix B. This number was net of subsidiaries.

For a given time period, there were four distinct groups of firms which emerged from combining the government's labor election records with financial statement databases, such as Compustat:

Classification	Description
D_w. Firms which have had union only decertification elections (union winning) in test period.	Net result: no change in membership.
D_l. Firms which have had only decertification elections (union losing) in test period.	Net result: decreasing union membership.
R_w. Firms which have had union only representation elections (union winning) in test period.	Net result: increasing membership.
R_l. Firms which have had only representation elections (union losing) in test period.	Net result: no change in union membership.
C. Firms listed only on Compustat but not on labor election tape.	Control group: union membership stable or company was union free.

Classification	Description

M. Firms that had multiple elections of differing types or differing results, i.e., they would not uniquely fit into D_w, D_l, R_w, R_l, or C.

Omitted from testing due to confounding effects.

This natural division of the firms lent itself well to a research design with four "experimental" groups: firms with decertification elections (D_w and D_l); firms with representation elections (R_w and R_l); and a control group (C) of publicly traded firms which were not identified in the labor elections files, which were controlled by industry at the four-digit SIC code level. There was a fourth group (M) of firms which reported either both types of elections or differing election results in the test period.

For purposes of selection and testing all observations were subject to a decision rule which required that any election be at least two years apart from any other election in the firm. While there were many elections, a majority either overlapped in time or were not far enough apart in time to allow testing of individual election effects. The net result of applying this rule was 181 observations for one year after the election and 129 observations for two years after the election, of which approximately 80 percent were the only elections known to have happened in the firm. The balance were a minimum of two years apart from any other election. The datasets for the one year post-election firms did not perfectly correspond to the two years post-election dataset. That is, there were firms with observations in both periods, firms with observations in the one year dataset but not the second year dataset, and firms with observations in the second year dataset but not the first year. This was a result of missing data in a period, or a missing control group in a period.

Observations tested were originally taken from the Compustat Industrial Annual file, as were firms used as controls for each of the observations. Subsequently, to enhance the pool of possible observations, testing was extended into the OTC Annual file. Firms in this file were also used as controls.

In the course of analysis it was observed that some observations reported an extreme or highly unusual value for at least one variable.

These were examined visually using data distributions and tables of the numerical values for largest and smallest observations. The issue was whether to keep the extreme observations in the dataset, or to discard them as outliers. Either keeping or discarding extreme observations could bias results. If an observation was not representative of the phenomenon being studied then it should be discarded, however if it was representative then it should be kept. The reliability of the actual numbers was a concern, since data entry errors in very large databases are not unknown. Afifi and Clark (1990, 37) noted that

> "Outliers are observations that appear inconsistent with the remainder of the dataset...Often, observations are obtained that seem quite high or low but are not impossible. These values are the most difficult ones to cope with. Should they be removed or not? Statisticians differ in their opinions, from "if in doubt, throw it out" to "the point of view that it is unethical to remove an outlier for fear of biasing the results. The investigator may wish to eliminate these outliers from the analyses but report them along with the statistical analysis."

Afifi and Clark (38) described a technique of visually screening data for outliers:

> "The data can be examined one variable at a time by using histograms if the variable is measured on the interval or ratio scale. A questionable value would be one that is separated from the remaining observations."

Examination of the data in question raised the issue of when some variables might not be reasonable, to wit: consider two firms which both used a sales force to market their products. In one, sales staff were all employees of the firm. In the other, the selling was done by self-employed factory representatives. In this hypothetical case, both firms would incur selling expense as a data item. However, the employee data item would not be comparable, because the factory representatives in one company would not be reported as employees. Thus the variable "sales per employee" will not be meaningfully comparable. To examine the effect of the outliers, the data were tested including the outliers and excluding the outliers. Appendix C contains information on these outliers. The next section discusses the research design.

THE RESEARCH DESIGN

The research design for this study was an equivalent time samples design (Campbell and Stanley 1966, 43). Figure III-1 depicts the different groups in the research design. A time-series design was ruled out because the subjects change each period. Original data on elections were only available from the NLRB on a monthly and annual basis. Daily data were not available. This mitigated against an event study. Further, the research question was directed at longer-term measures of firm performance, rather than cumulative abnormal returns which would have been the focus of an event study.

Observations selected for testing were compared to control groups. These corresponding control group consisted of those publicly traded Compustat firms which had not had either type of election in the entire twelve years of the test period and had the same SIC code and fiscal year-end as the firm being tested. As shown in Figure III-1 below, the O's were annual observations and D or R denoted the different types of elections. When a firm had an election, data were observed for the year before the election (O_b) and for the year after (O_a). The data for each firm which had a union election were compared with composite data for a control group of firms that were "union stable" (i.e., these firms had no elections) and in the same industry. To assure the greatest stability possible, Compustat firms were matched against all the company names in the labor files, and only firms not in the labor file were kept as possible controls. This control group strategy was similar to a matched pairs design, but all possible firms were used to create a composite control. This was intended to provide an industry match for the test observation. Consequently any given control group was composed of all available firms in the industry with the same year-end for which data could be obtained.

Figure III-1. Research design showing the outcomes over an equivalent time period for included companies.

Group Name	Election Timeline	Description
D_w	O_b D_w O_a	Decertifications - union won
D_l	O_b D_l O_a	Decertifications - union lost
R_w	O_b R_w O_a	Representations - union won
R_l	O_b R_l O_a	Representations - union lost
C	O_b $\sim D, \sim R$ O_a	No election of either type

Legend:

O_b = observations prior to elections.

O_a = observations after elections.

Test groups:

D_w = Decertification election won by union.

D_l = Decertification election lost by union.

R_w = Representation election won by union.

R_l = Representation election lost by union.

C = Control group:

$\sim D$ = no decertification election held.

$\sim R$ = no representation election held.

---

file. If the firm had any election during the period of 1977 through 1989, it was removed from the pool of possible controls. Empirical testing began with 1978 elections.

There were additional controls built into the design to strengthen the interpretation of any results. This study used annual Compustat data, as was done in a number of previous studies (Horwitz and Kolodny (1981), Imhoff (1981), Manegold (1981), Abdel-khalik (1985), and Lee (1985)). The use of annual data controlled for seasonal factors and year-end audit adjustments to financial data used as input. Harrison, Tomassini and Dietrich (1983, 66), in describing control group methodology, noted that control groups are used to control for the effects of history as an alternative explanation by using a control group

> "...which is exposed to the same confounding events, but not to the treatment. The maturation problem occurs when extraneous phenomena influence the dependent variable as a function of time. To control for these phenomena, a control group is used which is exposed to the same time-related phenomena."

The control group for each firm in this study was the group of Compustat firms in the same SIC code as the firm being tested (but which had not had election activity) for the same time periods. These firms were not included in any of the four groups with elections held in a given period. These firms, since they were not listed in the labor election files for union elections, were defined as being either union free or stable with respect to union variability. In that way, if they were unionized, they did not appear in the election data. This control group construction should have effectively controlled for the effects of history and maturation. For all firms, subsidiaries traded under separate names and CUSIP numbers were excluded.

After the observations were classified as shown in Figure III-1, financial data for each observation and control firm were obtained. The next sections explain the timing of elections and the collection of financial data for the related periods, and fiscal year-end issues.

MEASUREMENT

Data for testing were obtained by merging together two different datasets. Companies' labor election data were added to the individual firm-level financial statement data. Election data were recorded on a monthly basis and arrived at irregular times during the year; the elections may have been held at any time during the year. Company data were observed at regular year-end intervals as of December 31 of each year, or the end of the fiscal year. Thus for any given firm in the group, there were periods prior to the election and subsequent to the election.

When a union election occurred in the fourth quarter, it appeared unlikely that any measurable effect would be found by year-end. If a union election occurred in the fourth quarter of the firm's fiscal year, then it was considered as occurring in the first quarter of the following year. For example, if the election occurred in the fourth quarter of 1986, then that observation was matched to the financial data for 1987.

YEAR-END

Compustat included both calendar year-end and fiscal year-end firms. The following quotation describes Compustat's treatment of annual data for years ending January 1 through May 31:

Fiscal Year Codes (FYR)

This code designates the month-end for each company's accounting year. Fiscal years ending January 1 through May 31 are treated as ending in the prior calendar year. Thus, the data for a fiscal year beginning on June 1, 1984, and ending on May 31, 1985, would be reported as the year 1984; whereas a fiscal year beginning on July 1, 1984, and ending on June 30, 1985, would be reported as the year 1985. (Compustat manual, "Variable Definitions: Companies", Section 7-B, p.4, April 15, 1986.)

This issue was important in selection of firms for a given control group. To assure that the time period dimension was in fact held constant, every firm in a given control group was required to have the same month for its year-end as did the observation to which it was matched. This assured that all firms in a given test period were subject to the same general economic conditions. If the year-end requirement could not be met by at least one firm in the same industry, the observation was dropped, because there was no valid control group for that firm.

TESTING

The purpose of the tests was to identify differences in the changes in four variables (R&D spending, pension costs, return on investment, and productivity) before and after a union election, and compare these scores to a group of firms with no union election activity. Both univariate and multivariate testing were performed.

Univariate Testing

To determine whether there were differences in any variable between the test groups which had union elections and the control groups, a t-test of mean differences was performed. When the difference between the means of a test group and its control group was not equal to zero, this indicated an election effect. This test of mean differences was conducted for each variable independently of other variables.

An ANOVA was performed to test whether the means of a single measurement were equal across the four outcome groups. A two-way analysis of variance was performed to examine whether the variables were affected differently by type of election or by election outcome.

Multivariate Testing

When any of the union election outcome groups (test groups) differed from the others in the industry (control groups) then this indicated an election effect and one wished to know if there was any difference in the effects that accompanied the different union election outcomes. This difference was tested collectively for the four measures with a Multivariate Analysis of Variance (MANOVA) and individually for these four measures with univariate Analysis of Variance

(ANOVA). Figure III-2 shows the data structure of the difference measures for each of the outcome groups. The univariate tests previously described tested to determine if each of the sixteen differences were significantly different from zero. The null hypothesis associated with the MANOVA was that the mean vectors of differences for the four outcome groups were all equal. The null hypothesis was:

$$Ho: MV_{Dl} = MV_{Dw} = MV_{Rl} = MV_{Rw},$$

where:

  MV denotes the population vector of means for the measures of
  interest.

The multivariate testing generated four test procedures, including Wilks' lambda, Pillai's trace, Hotelling-Lawley trace, and Roy's maximum root. These tests produced p-values which were used as overall p-values to determine the significance of the multivariate test statistics.

Figure III-2. Data structure showing difference measurements for each outcome group.

| Outcome Groups | Measurements | | | |
	R&D	Pension	Profitability	Productivity
Decertification - union won				
Decertification - union lost				
Representation - union won				
Representation - union lost				

TECHNICAL ASPECTS OF THE
COMPUSTAT ANNUAL SERIES

The hypothesis testing just described relied on annual Compustat data, as have other studies (Abdel-khalik 1985, Horwitz and Kolodny 1981, Imhoff 1981, Lee 1985, and Manegold 1981). In addition to these, there are several specific arguments which highlight underlying reasons for using annual data series. These are presented based on relevance to the present study.

Data limitation - some annual items are not available quarterly.

Bao et al. (1983, 414) noted some data elements required for analysis were simply not available in any other form aside from annual: "It is important to recognize, however, that many of the variables used by Manegold (1981), or that may be desired by others, are not reported on a quarterly basis (e.g. gross investment, total debt, owners' equity and inventory)."

Beginning Availability of a Data Element

Directly affecting this study, Bublitz and Ettredge (1989) noted that sometimes a data element was simply not reported and was thus unavailable prior to the imposition of government-mandated reporting requirement for that element (in this case, annual R&D): "For most firms, annual data on advertising and R&D expenses are available on Compustat beginning about 1972 or 1973, probably because of a 1972 revision of Regulation S-X requiring these data to be reported to the Securities Exchange Commission as supplementary income statement information. The first year for which advertising and R&D forecast errors can be computed for a substantial number of firms is 1974..." (112, Note 8). Consequently there were limitations in how far into the past a study could effectively pursue R&D.

Reliability of Quarterly Estimates

Two of the variables used in this study, R&D and pension costs, were subject to potential measurement errors in quarterly data. Year-end preparation of financial statements and related audit adjustments may result in changes to previous quarters' estimates for variables of interest, such as R&D or pension/retirement costs, making the quarterly data unreliable. Bao (1983, 406) supports this: "Quarterly data are often not subject to detailed audit and may be influenced by more subjective measurement techniques than annual data." Bathke, Lorek and Willinger (1989, 67) discuss the "larger fourth quarter (forecast) errors" which Collins et al. (1984) had attributed to the "settling up or dumping effect by which accruals and deferrals on an interim basis are brought into correspondence with the annual numbers." Bathke et al. found that forecast errors in the fourth quarter depended on firm size: "Only the middle strata firms exhibited behavior consistent with this 'dumping' effect...". These concerns offered further support for the use of an annual data series.

Model Parsimony

Annual data represented an aggregation of quarterly or monthly data into annual amounts. The issue of how much information was lost when data were aggregated has been addressed by Cogger (1981, 296). Cogger noted that the use of annual numbers controlled for seasonal factors. In a test of specific firm data, the author found "...the relative efficiency of annual earnings is 0.89 with respect to quarterly" (earnings) if the interim quarterly data were not disclosed. This translated into an 11% information loss as the cost of using annual data rather than quarterly data. For purposes of this study, Cogger's results offer support for the use of annual data because the information loss was quite low. Since one annual observation summarizes four quarterly observations, the use of annual data reduced by 75% the number of observations needed to include sufficient years' data to obtain any possible evidence indicated in the hypotheses.

NOTES ON THE DATASET

The population of all organizations holding both possible types of union elections (representation and decertification) was available from the National Labor Relations Board (NLRB). The test dataset was created by matching the name of the firm from the NLRB's records with the Compustat file. If the name existed on both files, it entered the test file. The NLRB tape was not consistent with respect to company name format. A manual effort was made to correct the NLRB file of approximately 9,500 observations. This correction required manually checking the election data file against the Standard and Poor's *Register of Corporations, Directors, and Executives* for corroborating information on the correct company name and to match the address and Standard Industrial Classification (SIC) codes to those carried in the NLRB records. Further updating and correction of the NLRB data were carried out by obtaining approximately 300 company profiles through *Compact Disclosure* to determine current name, address, segment SIC codes, and merger/divestiture/bankruptcy data. The result of this effort, after discarding observations which could not be matched with a control group, or which did not have all data items available for all periods necessary, was a group of publicly traded firms which have experienced union elections during the period from 1978 to 1989, for which control groups could be established. This was the group tested in this study. There were 181 observations in the one year post-election dataset and 129 observations in the two year post-election dataset.

The merged dataset (containing both election data and financial data) was an input datafile for the SAS statistical package. All statistical analysis was completed using SAS.

CHAPTER SUMMARY

This chapter explained the research methodology, and the use of industry control groups. Research questions and the associated statistical hypotheses were developed. To test both individual variable changes and differences in mean vectors, univariate and multivariate test procedures were presented. Issues of measurement and fiscal year end were discussed. Research questions and the associated statistical hypotheses were developed. Support for the use of annual data was provided. The source of the dataset was explained, as were limitations and assumptions made.

The next chapter provides an analysis of the data. The last chapter summarizes the research and provides conclusions to the evidence found, and presents some avenues for future work.

IV

Presentation Of Data And
Analysis Of Findings

This chapter examines the results of empirical testing and provides analysis of the findings. Chapter V summarizes the research, presents conclusions reached, and suggests future avenues to extend the research.

FIRM SELECTION PROCEDURE

This research included publicly traded firms in the U.S. which had a labor union election between January 1978 and December 1989. Labor election data included all union elections held in the United States under the auspices of the National Labor Relations Board (NLRB). During this period nearly 70,000 labor elections were held. Financial data were taken from the Standard and Poor's Compustat Industrial and Over The Counter files. To be selected firms must not have experienced any other union elections within two years before or after the election event selected as an observation. This two year gap on either side of an election was chosen to provide a reasonable amount of time for any union effects of the prior (if any) election to be absorbed by the firm. Pakes (1985) reported a firm's R&D spending was influenced by environmental effects only if they had occurred within the previous three years. Pakes' results were used as a maximum time necessary for environmental effects to be incorporated into a firm. To accommodate as much time as possible between union elections and still obtain a reasonable number of observations, a gap of two years was selected.

Each firm observed was compared to a control group. The control group consisted of one or more publicly traded firms identified by Standard and Poor's Compustat as operating in the same standard industrial classification (SIC) code, and which had the same month as the fiscal year end. This was intended to control for industry effects and economic effects across the twelve years of data. While the original research proposal called for industry control by a three-digit SIC match, in practice it was possible to match nearly all observations using a four-digit SIC code. Eight observations required a three-digit match.

To be used in a control group, a company which met all preceding requirements must have had no union elections listed in the NLRB election file. This assured that firms used as controls were as stable in their union relations as was possible to determine. Observations which could not be matched with controls as described were discarded. There were 181 observations in the one year post-election dataset and 129 observations in the two year post-election dataset.

Initially, screening was performed as described in Chapter III to check for anomalies and outliers - observations which, although correctly recorded, were well beyond the customary distribution for the group in question, and whose inclusion would potentially bias the results. Visual screening was performed using stem-leaf distribution plots to identify such outliers. These were further verified through a numerical extreme values report. Observations deemed to be outliers were discarded.

The observations which were tested are described in Appendix B. Observations not retained in the dataset for analyses are identified in Appendix C.

To determine whether omitting observations would have changed any conclusions reached, testing was repeated upon the complete datasets, with no omissions. The univariate and multivariate results of this endeavor are reported at the back of this chapter under "Comparative univariate and multivariate tests."

To check the normality of the data, skewness was examined for the distributions. For data whose significance was marginal, the skewness test provided information about the normality of the data. Due to the results obtained, the skewness statistics did not affect any of the conclusions drawn from the analysis. Consequently skewness statistics were not reported.

As discussed in Chapter III, hypotheses testing was performed for a set of difference scores for the time period of one year pre-election to one year post-election, and for another set of difference scores for the time period of one year pre-election to two years post-election.

The number of complete observations that could be used in testing was:

	Differences	
	One Year Post-Election	Two Years Post-Election
Hypothesis 1 (Research and development)	n = 60	32
Hypothesis 2 (Pension and retirement expenses)	n = 113	68
Hypothesis 3 (Profitability)	n = 164	115
Hypothesis 4 (Productivity)	n = 176	116

The total number of observations represented in the datasets was 181 for the one year post-election group, and 129 for the two year post-election group.

The observations and control groups were compared on two measures of size, number of employees and total assets. As shown in Appendix D, no significant differences were found on either variable.

STATISTICAL TESTING

A series of analyses was performed. First, a "difference score" for each observation was calculated for each of four variables. The method of calculation is shown for each variable later in this chapter. The variables were R&D expenditures per employee, pension and retirement expenses per employee, profitability, and productivity. The difference score was defined as the company's (observation) score minus the industry's (control group) score for a given variable, over the test period. Second, four research questions listed below were asked.

Research Question 1

Were research and development expenditures on a per-employee basis significantly different between firms which have experienced a union election and those which have not?

Research Question 2

> Were pension and retirement expenses per employee significantly different between firms which have experienced a union election and those which have not?

Research Question 3

> Was profitability significantly different between firms which have experienced a union election and those which have not?

Research Question 4

> Was productivity, measured on the basis of sales per employee, significantly different between firms which have experienced a union election and those which have not?

If firms with union elections were different from their control groups, then the mean of the differences between the firms and the control groups would differ significantly from zero. A t-test was used to calculate a p-value to test each hypothesis.

Third, a two-way Analysis of Variance (ANOVA) was used to test if there were any differences between the types of election and/or outcome ("disposition") of the election. An ANOVA was conducted using the outcome variable for each of the four hypotheses. Univariate tests were chosen to determine whether there were differences between firms with elections and the control group firms without elections on each of the four variables: 1) sales per employee, 2) pension and retirement expenditures per employee, 3) research and development spending per employee, and 4) return on investment. Finally a Multivariate Analysis of Variance (MANOVA) was conducted to determine if there were any overall effects clearly present. The MANOVA tested for differences in the mean vector of one group of companies compared to another group of companies. The MANOVA procedure examined all variables simultaneously, as opposed to each variable individually. The General Linear Model in the SAS package was used, testing whether there were significant differences in the mean vectors between types of elections and/or between dispositions. The General Linear Model (GLM) procedure which was used required a value to be present for all variables for each observation in order for that observation to be included in the test. Consequently, this multivariate test dropped observations which were lacking at least one of either research and development costs, or pension costs, or return on investment, or sales. The multivariate testing produced p-values from four tests, including Wilks' lambda, Pillai's trace, Hotelling-Lawley trace, and Roy's maximum root. These were used to generate an overall p-value which was used to determine the significance of the multivariate test statistics.

PRESENTATION OF DATA AND RESULTS

Research Question 1

The hypothesis resulting from research question 1 tested whether there were differences in annual per-employee research and development (R&D) expenses, between companies which have had union elections and those firms in the control groups which have not had union elections during the test period.

The t-test statistic was computed as follows:
DD1 = the difference in per-employee research and development expenses between the company and its industry control group for the period one year prior to the election to one year post-election. This was computed as below for each test observation, with a result termed DD1, and was computed for each control group, with a result termed MD1:

$$\frac{R\&D_{E+1}}{(EMP_E + EMP_{E+1})/2} - \frac{R\&D_{E-1}}{(EMP_{E-1} + EMP_{E-2})/2} = DD1.$$

where:

R&D = research and development spending; EMP = employees at the year-end; and E refers to the election year for the data variable. Per-employee variables were computed with an average number of employees which was the previous year's employee count plus the current year's employee count divided by two.

Next the difference between the two scores was calculated:
DiffR&D1 = DD1 - MD1.

The firm's resulting score was called DD1; for the control group the score was called MD1. Subtracting the industry score MD1 from the observation score DD1 yielded a difference score termed DiffR&D1. If there were a significant difference between the means of DD1 and MD1, then there would be a difference in per-employee research and development spending between firms with union elections and those without union elections. To answer the research question, the following hypothesis was tested.

Ho^1: DiffR&D1 = 0.
Ha^1: DiffR&D1 $\neq$ 0.

Since it was not possible to predict the direction of the test results, a two-tailed test was used. The test was repeated for a second dataset, for the differences calculated two years after the election. Table IV-1 presents the results of the t-test of means for this hypothesis, for both one year post-election and two years post-election. The related multivariate tests appear in Tables IV-17, IV-18, and IV-19.

As shown in Table IV-1, neither of the univariate results for the test of R&D spending were significant at the .05 level. The p-value for the two years post-election test would be significant at the .10 level. This was interpreted to mean that there was no significant difference in the change in R&D spending between the observation group and the control groups after one year, but the statistics suggest that there is a difference after two years.

Table IV-1. Univariate test results for differences in per-employee R&D expenditures for test group vs. control group.

	One Year Post-Election	Two Years Post-Election
Sample size	60	32
H1: Mean $\neq$ 0		
Statistic	-0.192	-1.744
P-value	0.849	0.091

In addition the data were partitioned in three different ways to explore other possible relationships. The rationale for the partitioning is presented along with results being presented in each of the next three tables.

Table IV-2 shows the results of partitioning the data by type of election, for the period one year pre-election to one year post-election. This test explained whether firms which the union was attempting to organize through representation elections spent more or less per employee than firms in which the union was exiting (dependent upon the election outcome). Testing for difference by election type provided no significant results. The resulting test statistic for representation elections was of a different sign than that of the statistic for decertification elections. Both p-values were extremely high, which did not support a shift in means.

Table IV-2. Univariate test of per-employee R&D expenditures by election type, one year prior to the election compared to one year post-election.

	Representation Elections	Decertification Elections
Sample size	37	23
H1: Mean ≠ 0		
Statistic	-0.362	0.020
P-value	0.720	0.984

The next univariate test for research and development was to determine if there were differences in per-employee R&D expenditures depending on whether the union won or lost the election. This included both representation and decertification elections. The results obtained are presented in Table IV-3.

Table IV-3 shows that the p-value was considerably lower for union wins (.19) than union losses (.75) but these were in excess of alpha. In summary, however, this test did not return significant results.

Table IV-3. Univariate test of per-employee R&D expenditures by disposition, one year prior to the election compared to one year post-election.

	Union Won	Union Lost
Sample size	22	38
H1: Mean $\neq$ 0		
Statistic	-1.335	0.311
P-value	0.196	0.757

The final test of research and development spending was a univariate t-test for each of four possibilities: representation elections the union won, representation elections the union lost, decertification elections the union won, and decertification elections the union lost. These results appear in Table IV-4.

Table IV-4. Univariate test of per-employee R&D expenditures by election type and disposition, one year prior to the election compared to one year post-election.

	Representation Elections		Decertification Elections	
	Union Won	Union Lost	Union Won	Union Lost
Sample size	15	22	7	16
H1: Mean $\neq$ 0				
Statistic	-1.551	-0.007	-0.793	0.388
P-value	0.143	0.995	0.458	0.703

Finally, the fully partitioned R&D dataset (Table IV-4) decomposed the data but again the results were not significant. The test statistics were negative, except for decertification elections which the union lost. Previous studies reviewed in Chapter II suggested that in cases of union wins, R&D spending would be below the mean. As expected, in both cases of union wins, R&D spending was below the mean. Only in representation elections the union won does the p-value approach significance. Overall, this test indicated that one could anticipate different levels of R&D spending to be related to the type and disposition of election. The summary is that these were not significant results.

Research Question 2

The hypothesis developed from the second research question tested whether per-employee pension and retirement expenses were significantly different between firms which had experienced a union election and those which had not.

The t-test statistic was computed as follows:
DP1 = the difference in per-employee research and development expenses between the company and its industry control group for the period one year prior to the election to one year post election. This was computed as below for each test observation, with a result termed DP1. It was computed for each control group and termed MP1.

$$\frac{PRS_{E+1}}{(EMP_E + EMP_{E+1})/2} - \frac{PRS_{E-1}}{(EMP_{E-1} + EMP_{E-2})/2} = DP1$$

where:
PRS = pension and retirement spending; EMP = employees at the year-end; and E refers to the election year for the data variable. Per-employee variables were computed with an average number of employees which was the previous year's employee count plus the current year's employee count divided by two.

Next the difference between the two scores was calculated:
DiffPEN1 = DP1 - MP1.

The firm's resulting score was called DP1; for the control group the score was called MP1. Subtracting the industry score MP1 from the observation score DP1 yielded a difference score termed DiffPEN1. If there were a significant difference between the means of DP1 and MP1, then there would be a difference in per-employee pension and retirement expenditures between firms with union elections and those without union elections. To answer the research question, the following hypothesis was tested.

Ho^2: DiffPEN1 = 0.
Ha^2: DiffPEN1 $\neq$ 0.

Since it was not possible to predict the direction of the test results, a two-tailed test was used. The test was repeated for a second dataset, for the differences calculated two years after the election. This hypothesis was tested five years post-election also, to determine whether longer time lags might be useful to identify differences in pension and retirement spending.

Table IV-5 presents the results of the t-test of means for this hypothesis, for three time periods. Related multivariate tests appear in Tables IV-17, IV-18, and IV-19.

Table IV-5. Univariate test results for per-employee pension and retirement expenditures, test group vs. control group.

	One Year Post-Election	Two Years Post-Election	Five Years Post-Election
Sample size	121	68	20
H2: Mean $\neq$ 0			
Statistic	1.899	0.989	0.313
P-value	0.060	0.326	0.757

The t-test of mean differences being equal to zero indicated that in the one year post-election measure, the mean of pension spending for all firms with elections was positive and considerably above that of the control groups, which had no union elections. The p-value was significant at the .10 level. While the one year post-election test provided a substantial amount of explanatory power for increased pension spending, the same test two years after the election provided very little explanatory power. The t-test of means was still positive the second year, but not nearly as high as the first year. Because the p-value was .06 for the results of one year post-election, the hypothesis of no significant differences in pension and retirement expenditures may not be rejected at the alpha =.05 level. As noted earlier, this hypothesis was tested again five years after the election (Table IV-5) to determine whether a longer lag time was necessary to capture changes in the levels of spending for pension and retirement benefits.

As the results indicate, this was not found to be the case. The p-value for the significance of the test statistic was high enough that no explanatory power can be attached to this longer term test.

The data were subjected to additional testing to probe any further differences. Univariate tests were conducted by election type, by disposition, and by both election type and disposition. These are presented in the same format as was used for Hypothesis 1, and appear in Tables IV-6, IV-7, and IV-8.

Table IV-6. Univariate test results for per-employee pension and retirement expenditures by disposition, one year prior to the election compared to one year post-election.

	Union Won	Union Lost
Sample size	44	77
H2: Mean $\neq$ 0		
Statistic	1.631	1.216
P-value	0.110	0.228

Testing pension expenses by whether the union won or lost the election (disposition) would presumably indicate higher pension spending in firms where unions won elections, due to contract negotiations for increased pension and retirement benefits. Table IV-6 does indicate that the mean of the spending per employee was higher in firms where the union won either type of election. The p-values obtained were not significant at the .10 alpha level, however. It is worth noting that simply having a union election may indicate higher pension costs than in firms with no union elections, as may be seen in Tables IV-5, IV-6, IV-7, and IV-8. In all cases, the test statistics were positive.

Test results by election type are detailed in Table IV-7. Partitioning by election type provided more insight than did partitioning by wins and losses. The mean of spending for per-employee pensions

Table IV-7. Univariate test results for per-employee pension and retirement expenditures by election type, one year prior to the election compared to one year post-election.

	Representation Elections	Decertification Elections
Sample size	78	43
H2: Mean ≠ 0		
Statistic	1.698	0.855
P-value	0.094	0.398

in firms with representation elections was two times that of firms with decertification elections. The p-value for decertification elections one year after the election was .398, which was not significant. The p-value for representation elections was .094 which was significant at the .10 alpha level.

The fully partitioned test of per-employee pension and retirement expenditures is presented in Table IV-8. Again, the means of spending for pension and retirement were positive compared to the control groups with no elections. In this set there was some difference in the means because representation elections showed higher per-employee spending than did non-electing control firms, and the means of representation elections were higher than decertification elections. The p-values were lower for representation elections than for decertification elections; none were significant at the .05 level. It appears there was a difference due to the fact that elections were held, but the marginal significance found was not sufficient to reject the hypothesis of no

Table IV-8.   Univariate test results for per-employee pension and retirement expenditures by election type and disposition, one year prior to the election compared to one year post-election.

	Representation Elections		Decertification Elections	
	Union Won	Union Lost	Union Won	Union Lost
Sample size	28	50	16	27
H2: Mean $\neq$ 0				
Statistic	1.445	1.114	0.758	0.492
P-value	0.160	0.271	0.460	0.627

difference in per-employee spending for pensions.

Research Question 3

The hypothesis developed from the third research question tested whether profitability, defined as return on investment (net income divided by total assets), was significantly different between firms which had experienced a union election and those which had not.

The t-test statistic was computed in the same manner as for the two previous hypotheses. A set of difference scores was generated, computed as follows: DR1 = the difference in return on investment (ROI) measured at one year prior to the election (E-1), subtracted from the measurement at one year after the election (E+1), for the observation firm (with the result termed DR1), and for the control group (with the result termed MR1):

$$\frac{\text{Net income}_{E+1}}{\text{Total assets}_{E+1}} - \frac{\text{Net income}_{E-1}}{\text{Total assets}_{E-1}} = DR1.$$

where:
E refers to the election year for the data variable.

Next the difference between the two scores was calculated:
DiffROI1 = DR1 - MR1.

These were used to generate the difference score DiffROI1, which was the company change - the industry change. If there was a significant difference between the means of DR1 and MR1, then there existed a difference in return on investment between firms with union elections and those firms without union elections. The hypothesis tested to answer this research question was:

Ho³: DiffROI1 = 0.
Ha³: DiffROI1 ≠ 0.

The direction of the change was not known in advance; hence a two-tailed test was performed. The test was performed again on a second dataset, for the differences calculated two years after the election. The results of the univariate t-test of means for Hypothesis 3 are shown in Table IV-9. The multivariate test results for this variable are presented in Tables IV-17, IV-18, and IV-19.

Table IV-9. Univariate test results for return on investment, for test group vs. control group.

	One Year Post-Election	Two Years Post-Election
Sample size	168	116
H3: Mean ≠ 0		
Statistic	-0.076	1.115
P-value	0.940	0.267

None of the univariate results for the test of return on investment were significant. The p-values were high for both periods so the statistic was not significant. The null hypothesis of no difference between union and nonunion firms could not be rejected.

In order to probe further and determine if partitioning the data would uncover any relationships, exploratory testing of return on investment by election type and election outcome was done. These results are reported in Tables IV-10, IV-11, and IV-12.

Table IV-10. Univariate test results for return on investment by election type, one year prior to the election compared to one year post-election.

	Representation Elections	Decertification Elections
Sample size	100	68
H3: Mean $\neq$ 0		
Statistic	0.078	-0.146
P-value	0.938	0.884

Table IV-10 shows that the p-values were above those required for significance at a .05 level.

Table IV-11. Univariate test results for return on investment by disposition, one year prior to the election compared to one year post-election.

	Union Won	Union Lost
Sample size	71	97
H3: Mean $\neq$ 0		
Statistic	-0.674	0.244
P-value	0.503	0.808

Table IV-11 reports the test of return on investment by election outcome. The negative sign on the test statistic for elections the union won was supported by prior studies. However, the p-values were sufficiently high, so that this test did not produce significant findings.

Finally, the fully partitioned ROI sample was tested for differences by election type and election outcome.

Table IV-12. Univariate test results for return on investment by election type and disposition, one year prior to the election compared to one year post-election.

	Representation Elections		Decertification Elections	
	Union Won	Union Lost	Union Won	Union Lost
Sample size	41	59	30	38
H3: Mean $\neq$ 0				
Statistic	-0.070	0.145	-0.946	0.195
P-value	0.944	0.885	0.352	0.846

Results are given in Table IV-12. In both election types which unions won, the test statistic was negative compared to the control groups. Where unions lost either type of election, the test statistic was positive. However, no significance can be attached to these results due to the high p-values.

Research Question 4

The hypothesis resulting from research question 4 tested whether productivity, measured on the basis of per-employee sales, was significantly different between firms which have experienced a union election and those which have not. The t-test statistic was calculated as follows. DS1 = the difference in per-employee sales between the company and its industry control group for the period one year prior to the election to one year post-election. This was computed as for

$$\frac{\text{Net Sales}_{E+1}}{(\text{EMP}_E + \text{EMP}_{E+1})/2} - \frac{\text{Net Sales}_{E-1}}{(\text{EMP}_{E-1} + \text{EMP}_{E-2})/2} = \text{DS1}$$

each test observation, and MS1 for each control group observation, where:

EMP = employees at the year-end; and E refers to the election year for the data variable. Per-employee variables were computed with an average number of employees which was the previous year's employee count plus the current year's employee count divided by two.

Next the difference between the two scores was calculated: DiffSALES1 = DS1 - MS1.

A significant difference between the means of DS1 and MS1 would indicate a difference in per-employee sales between firms with union elections and those without union elections. The hypothesis which was tested to provide an answer to this research question was:

Ho^4: DiffSALES1 = 0.
Ha^4: DiffSALES1 ≠ 0.

It was not possible to predict in advance the direction of the change, therefore a two-tailed test was used. The test was performed a second time on the two year post-election dataset. The univariate results are presented in Table IV-13. Multivariate test results for this variable are shown beginning with Table IV-17.

Table IV-13. Univariate test results for per-employee sales, for test group vs. control group.

	One Year Post-Election	Two Years Post-Election
Sample size	178	115
H4: Mean ≠ 0		
Statistic	0.823	-0.922
P-value	0.412	0.358

Univariate results of testing per-employee sales produced insignificant results. Both of the p-values were in excess of reasonable alpha levels, so the test statistics did not provide us with new information. The data were partitioned and tested separately to identify any relationships not identifiable in previous testing. These results are described in Tables IV-14, IV-15, and IV-16.

Table IV-14. Univariate test of per-employee sales by election type, one year prior to the election compared to one year post-election.

	Representation Elections	Decertification Elections
Sample size	106	72
H4: Mean $\neq$ 0		
Statistic	0.925	0.238
P-value	0.357	0.812

Testing the partitioned dataset for per-employee sales did not yield significant results when tested by type of election (Table IV-14). Both p-values were in excess of the .10 alpha level. The next test was by disposition.

Table IV-15. Univariate test of per-employee sales by disposition, one year prior to the election compared to one year post-election.

	Union Won	Union Lost
Sample size	76	102
H4: Mean $\neq$ 0		
Statistic	-1.060	1.937
P-value	0.292	0.055

Table IV-15 presents the test of sales by disposition. This variable was annual sales divided by the average number of employees in the firm for that year. The test statistic was high and positive (1.937) for union losses compared to a negative (-1.060) in cases where unions won elections. This was significant at the .10 alpha level (p-value = 0.055).

The variable per-employee sales was tested by type and disposition. Results appear in Table IV-16. This encompassed all four possibilities: representation elections the union won, representation elections the union lost, decertification elections the union won, and decertification elections the union lost.

Testing the fully partitioned sales dataset for each subgroup (Table IV-16) provided some insight but results were not significant at the .05 alpha level. For decertification elections which the union won, the mean of per-employee sales was significantly below the mean for non-electing control firms, at the .10 alpha level. Other categories of elections did not provide significant results.

Table IV-16. Univariate test of per-employee sales by election type and disposition, one year prior to the election compared to one year post-election.

| | Representation Elections | | Decertification Elections | |
	Union Won	Union Lost	Union Won	Union Lost
Sample size	45	61	31	41
H4: Mean $\neq$ 0				
Statistic	0.058	1.192	-1.720	1.529
P-value	0.954	0.238	0.096	0.134

This concluded the first step in testing the hypotheses. The next step in testing procedures used a two-way analysis of variance (ANOVA) to test for differences between election type and election disposition. An ANOVA was performed for each of the four variables, with the results shown in Tables IV-17 and IV-18. Discussion follows the second table.

Table IV-17. Two-way ANOVA test results for one year pre-election to one year post-election.

Variable	N	Disposition P-value	Type P-Value
Pensions	121	0.725	0.641
R&D	60	0.406	0.855
Sales	178	0.040	0.738
ROI	168	0.597	0.856

The next table presents the two years post-election test results.

Table IV-18. Two-way ANOVA test results for one year pre-election to two years post-election.

Variable	N	Disposition P-value	Type P-Value
Pensions	68	0.004	0.361
R&D	32	0.377	0.073
Sales	115	0.494	0.989
ROI	116	0.039	0.023

        As indicated in Table IV-17, the ANOVA procedure did not identify any explanatory power in the pension or R&D variables, but at the .05 level per-employee sales was significant for the one year post-election test. This result was consistent with the univariate test of sales. However, performing the same test for the two years post-election data yielded almost the reverse effect - sales had a high p-value. Table IV-18 for the two years post-election data indicates that pensions and ROI had low p-values (significant at .01 and .05 alpha, respectively) for the "disposition" variable. Research and development expenditures were found to be significantly different, at the .10 alpha level, from the non-electing control firms on the election "type" variance. Return on investment was significantly different in firms with union elections, at the .05 alpha level, from non-electing firms. In this case ROI was sensitive on both dimensions to the election event.
        The multivariate test used a MANOVA to test for differences between types of elections or between dispositions. The MANOVA can only process observations with all four variables. Forty-four observations were used for the one year post-election dataset. The two years post-election dataset contained 25 observations.
        None of the results were significant. All p-values reported were in excess of the .10 alpha level. This test indicated that neither election disposition or type offered any real significant explanatory power in a multivariate test.
        Earlier it was noted the p-values used for determining significance of the multivariate statistics were obtained from the individual p-values generated by four test procedures in the MANOVA. The p-values

listed in Table IV-19 were the p-values reported by all four of the procedures. For both the one year post-election test, and the two year post-election test, the same p-value was obtained from each of the four procedures. Therefore, only a single p-value is shown in the table.

Table IV-19. MANOVA results for one year post-election and for two years post-election.

Period	Variable	Results
One Year:	Disposition	P-value = 0.493
	Type	P-value = 0.560
Two Years:	Disposition	P-value = 0.497
	Type	P-value = 0.394

The results of the multivariate testing were not significant. Although significance was obtained in the univariate test procedures, the magnitude of any differences was not sufficient to be detected when tested in a multivariate test.

This concludes the discussion of test results obtained using data which had been screened for outliers. Testing was performed again on the complete dataset, which had no outliers removed. The results of this testing are compared to the prior results in next section of the chapter.

COMPARATIVE UNIVARIATE AND MULTIVARIATE TESTS

Comparative Univariate Tests With and Without Outliers

In case someone questioned the reasonableness of omitting outliers from the analysis, the full dataset was run with all observations to determine whether the results might differ from those results which were obtained using data from which the outliers had been removed. The observations which were removed in the original analysis are reported in Appendix C along with support for them being considered as outliers.

Analysis of the one year pre-election to one year post-election dataset with no outliers omitted generated the results in the tables that follow. For contrast, the appropriate values from the original analysis are reproduced on the right of the new results.

The first hypothesis tested for differences in expenditures for research and development and the results are in Table IV-20.

Table IV-20.   Comparative univariate test results for differences in per-employee research and development expenditures.

	One Year Post-Election Dataset with no Omissions	One Year Post-Election Dataset with Outliers Removed
Sample size	62	60
H1: Mean $\neq$ 0		
Statistic	-0.251	-0.192
P-value	0.803	0.849

Two observations had been removed from the one year post-election analysis for Hypothesis 1. Although including the additional observations increased the test statistic, the decrease in the p-value was not a major change.

The second hypothesis tested for differences in pension and retirement expenditures on a per-employee basis. There were no observations removed from the one year post-election dataset for pension and retirement expenditures. No comparative table is needed.

Table IV-21.   Comparative univariate test results for differences in return on investment.

	One Year Post-Election Dataset with no Omissions	One Year Post-Election Dataset with Outliers Removed
Sample size	171	168
H3: Mean $\neq$ 0		
Statistic	-0.656	-0.076
P-value	0.513	0.940

Table IV-21 displays results of comparative testing for Hypothesis 3, regarding profitability. Three observations were removed for the test of return on investment. The observations removed all had negative values (see Appendix C). Removal of these resulted in a more negative mean difference compared to the control groups. The p-value changed, by including the outliers, but the results obtained remained insignificant.

Table IV-22. Comparative univariate test results for differences in per-employee sales.

	One Year Post-Election Dataset with no Omissions	One Year Post-Election Dataset with Outliers Removed
Sample size	181	178
H4: Mean $\neq$ 0		
Statistic	1.216	0.823
P-value	0.225	0.412

The fourth hypothesis tested per-employee sales. Three observations were removed for the one year post-election test of sales per average employee (see Appendix C). Table IV-22 indicates that larger mean differences exist in the unscreened data, due to the large values associated with the three observations omitted. As the comparative data indicate, removal had no impact on the conclusions reached.

Table IV-23 presents the results of the Analysis of Variance tests with and without the outliers. The comparative data from screened versus unscreened ANOVA testing indicates changes from omission of the outliers. Variables are discussed in order of appearance in the table.

Table IV-23. Comparative two-way ANOVA test results for one year pre-election to one year post-election, with screening and without.

Variable	N	One Year Post-Election Dataset with no Omissions		N	One Year Post-Election Dataset with Outliers Removed	
		Disposition P-value	Type P-value		Disposition P-value	Type P-value
Pensions	121	0.725	0.641	121*	0.725	0.641
R&D	62	0.617	0.176	60	0.402	0.855
Sales	181	0.151	0.452	178	0.040	0.738
ROI	171	0.077	0.865	168	0.597	0.856

* No observations were removed for this variable.

Pensions

No observations were removed for the per-employee pension and retirement expenditures variable.

Research and Development (R&D)

Analysis of unscreened data generated a substantial change in the p-value for analysis of variance by "type of election". The screened data yielded a p-value of 0.855; the unscreened p-value was 0.176. However, the conclusions for this test would not change with the results remaining insignificant.

Sales

"Type of election" generated high p-values in either case with no change in conclusions. The "disposition" or outcome of the election showed a change. The p-value for the screened data was 0.040, significant at the .05 alpha level, but increased to 0.151 when unscreened data were analyzed.

Return on Investment (ROI)

Comparison of ANOVA results for screened versus unscreened data showed consistent results for the "disposition" as an explanation of variance. The original test of screened data yielded a p-value of 0.597, which was not significant at the .10 alpha level. The same test for unscreened data generated a p-value of 0.077, which was significant at the .10 alpha level. The "type of election" showed virtually no change when unscreened data were used (p-value = 0.865), compared to screened data results (p-value = 0.856).

In summary, ROI was significantly different from the control groups when unscreened data were used. Sales was significantly different from the control groups when screened data were used. This movement in p-values was due to three values in each case, which reinforces a conclusion that they are representing something different from the other data (168 and 178 observations respectively).

Comparative Multivariate Testing With and Without Outliers

The one year post-election dataset was analyzed with outliers included to determine whether screening had affected the results obtained from the MANOVA procedures.

The results are reported below.

Table IV-24. Comparative MANOVA test results for one year pre-election to one year post-election, with screening and without.

One Year Post-Election Dataset With no Omissions		One Year Post-Election Dataset With Outliers Removed	
Variable	Result	Variable	Result
Disposition	P-value = 0.478	Disposition	P-value = 0.493
Type	P-value = 0.389	Type	P-value = 0.560
N	45	N	44

Analysis using all observations yielded slightly changed p-values for both "disposition" of election and "type of election" as causes of variance. The change in the p-value for "disposition" was modest (from 0.493 screened to 0.478 unscreened). The change in the p-value for "type of election" was larger (decreasing from 0.560 to 0.389 for unscreened data). However, the conclusions were consistent with the original MANOVA test results. Neither case was significant.

SUMMARY OF THE CHAPTER

This chapter reported the results of data collection and analysis. Four research questions were statistically tested in both univariate and multivariate procedures to identify changes in four variables associated with union elections.

Per-employee research and development expenditures were significantly affected by union elections at the .10 alpha level two years after an election (Table IV-1).

Per-employee pension and retirement expenditures were significantly affected, at the .10 alpha level, by union elections one year after the election. This was not found to be the case for data either two years or five years after the election, however (Table IV-5). Pension costs for all representation elections were significantly higher at the .10 alpha level than those in the control groups (Table IV-7).

Return on investment was not found to be significantly different in firms with union elections, compared to firms without union elections.

For elections the union lost, per-employee sales was significantly higher at the .10 alpha level for firms with elections than for control groups with no elections (Table IV-15). Decertification elections won by unions had per-employee sales significantly lower than for the corresponding control groups with no elections, at the .10 alpha level. The difference from before the election to after the election was negative in this case.

The ANOVA tested whether the election effect was the same for all subgroups. If no election effect were present, the differences between the groups would have been zero. Table IV-17 indicated that there was an election effect based on the disposition of the election for the per-employee sales variable for the period ending one year after the election. The ANOVA performed for data two years after an election (Table IV-18) provided results differing from those obtained from the one year ANOVA. An election effect was found for the per-employee pension variable, which varied significantly for the two year data at the .01 alpha level, based on the disposition of the election. R&D was found to vary significantly for the election type variable at the .10 alpha level, for the two year data. Finally, ROI was significantly different at the .05 alpha level for both the election disposition variable and the election type variable, in the two year data but not in the one year data.

The MANOVA procedure did not identify significant results. This was an indication that the magnitudes of the results obtained for individual variables were not enough to be identified as significant when all four variables were considered together.

The fifth chapter provides a summary for the study. It also discusses conclusions drawn, limitations found, and proposes some directions for future work in this area.

V

Summary, Conclusions, And Limitations

This chapter provides a summary of the results of the data analysis. The conclusions drawn from this research are discussed. Limitations of this research and some possible directions for future efforts are identified.

The objective of this study was to determine whether current accounting requirements for disclosure of information to investors and analysts would be improved by including labor union election data in the set of required disclosures.

To satisfy this objective a dataset of all union elections identified with publicly traded firms in the Standard & Poor's Compustat data file was created. Four research questions were examined. The first of these was whether research and development expenditures on a per-employee basis were significantly different in firms with union elections, compared to firms with no union elections. The second question asked if pension and retirement expenses on a per-employee basis were different in firms with union elections, compared to firms without union elections. The third question asked whether there were significant differences in profitability in firms with union elections compared to firms without union elections. The last question was whether there existed differences in productivity, measured on the basis of sales per employee, in firms with union elections compared to firms without union elections.

To minimize general economic differences and industry differences over time, each observation was compared to a unique control group of firms in the same SIC code with the same fiscal year-end. Control group firms had no identifiable union elections during the period of the tests. Each of these research questions is summarized below.

RESEARCH QUESTION 1

The first research question focused on whether research and development expenditures on a per-employee basis were different in firms with union elections compared to firms in the same industry which had not had union elections.

Research and development spending as a disclosure item has been identified as important to investors (Buzby, 1974) and to analysts and users of financial statements (Chandra, 1974). Empirical testing of research and development at the industry level was presented in Connolly, Hirsch, and Hirschey (1986) and at the firm level in Hirsch (1992). The current study tested research and development spending for the differences in expenditures per employee for a period from one year before the election to one year after and for a period of one year before the election to two years afterward. None of the univariate t-tests generated significant results when measured at an alpha level of .05, but for the second year post-election, the results obtained were significant at the .10 alpha level. The test statistic indicated that in the second year post-election, firms with elections would spend $1,744 less per employee, compared to the control group with no elections. The negative test statistic was consistent with the first year's sign. The downward trend of the p-value suggests that a longer-term test of the differences in R&D spending might provide significant results. Performing a two-way ANOVA test on election outcome and election type on both datasets (one year post-election and two years post-election) provided significant results in the two year data. The election type variable was significantly different for R&D in firms with elections, compared to firms without elections, at the .10 alpha level. The multivariate results are discussed after each individual univariate test.

Both Connolly, Hirsch, and Hirschey (1986) and Hirsch (1992) reported significant decreases in R&D spending as unionization increased. The study by Connolly, Hirsch, and Hirschey (1986) differed from the current one in that they tested a different population of firms (367 firms in the 1977 Fortune 500) at an earlier time. The union variable in their prior study was a predicted percentage of employees in a firm who were union members in the firm's primary three-digit Census industry. Hirsch (1992) reported significant decreases in R&D spending in unionized firms, compared to nonunion peers. Hirsch's study used union or nonunion firm status as the independent variable, segmented by percent organized, and was limited to publicly traded manufacturing firms, for an earlier period (1972-1980).

The present study used the union election to indicate a change in the level of unionization of firms, for a later time period, using four-digit SIC codes for the industry control. It is possible that similar results might have been obtained if the current study had been restricted to Fortune 500 firms using different union variables. Although significant results at an alpha of .05 were not obtained in this test, it is worth noting that the direction of the results obtained in the current study were the same as in the previous studies. The mean of the difference between electing firms and non-electing firms was -$1,335 for elections the union won, and +$311 in firms in which the union lost the election. This supports the idea that research and development spending was lower in firms with labor elections than in firms without labor elections.

Another dimension of R&D spending is whether, as suggested above, there might be a time lag necessary to capture significant results. Pakes (1985) found that environmental changes occurring within three years or less of a change in R&D spending led to the firm's changing its R&D spending. This suggested that a three year time frame might be necessary to capture changes influencing R&D spending, and conversely suggested that one or two years post-election may not be sufficient time to measure the changes in spending. Another aspect of R&D spending which was not contemplated in this study was how far in advance research and development budgets are set by firms. This is an item over which firm management has much more discretion than some other variables, such as sales.

RESEARCH QUESTION 2

The second research question considered whether there were changes in per-employee spending for pension and retirement benefits in firms with union elections, compared to firms without union elections. The motivation for selecting this variable as a potential addition to the disclosure information set again came from earlier disclosure research (Buzby, 1974) as well as empirical work (Freeman, 1981). Freeman, using data from 1967 - 1972, found that pension expenses were two to three times higher in union firms than in nonunion firms. Results obtained in the present study support this earlier work. In this book, the mean difference between pension spending for all firms with elections, compared to the control group with no elections, was positive and significantly different from zero, at +$1,899 per employee. This was for the test of differences one year post-election, significant at the .10 alpha level. This is comparable to an estimate of the union compensation difference by Becker and Olson (1992). That study provided a calculation of the pretax union compensation (wages and benefits) difference of $2,294 for their sample.

This study did not find any significant results for pensions when tested two years after the election. A two-way analysis of variance was performed for the one year post-election dataset and for the two year post-election dataset. The results of this were not significant for the one year post-election data. For the data two years post-election, however, the results were significant at the .01 alpha level for the election disposition variable. A five year lagged test was performed to determine if pension benefits, which are bargainable issues with union membership during contract talks, would require longer than one or two years to generate identifiable differences in the financial statements. This was not found to be significant. Thus, it appeared that one year post-election was sufficient time for changes in this variable to make their way to the income statement. The data also suggested that pension and retirement expenditures were sensitive to which party won the election.

What was perhaps most striking for the pension variable was that in all cases, the test statistic was positive, compared to the control groups with no elections. The fact that an election had been held, regardless of type or outcome, was sufficient to increase this variable above that of non-electing firms. These results were not always significant but they were consistently uniform in direction.

The hypotheses concerning pension and retirement spending and research and development spending were operationalized by variables which are more controllable by the firm than are sales and return on investment. Pension and retirement benefits are a normal part of contract bargaining. Because this expenditure was subject to a firm's decision if the firm was nonunion, and was a negotiated item if the firm had a union, this cost was much more controllable by the firm. The economic environment would have less direct influence on this cost. Thus, if significant differences were to be found they should have occurred in an area controllable directly by the firm and/or labor union. This was the case with the elections won by labor unions. In both representation and decertification elections which the union won, the mean difference of pension and retirement costs was greater than in the elections which they lost. The mean difference was approximately one-third higher in union-won elections than in union-lost elections ($1,631 versus $1,216). This suggests that this element of a firm's compensation package and total cost was higher in firms which have had union elections than those firms which have not had union elections.

Since this variable presents significant differences in costs between firms with elections and firms not having elections, the issue of disclosure of this event should be addressed by the accounting profession. It was noted in the literature review that prior research had suggested that users and analysts of financial statements would favor disclosure of pension costs. However, because of rules for recognition of transactions, contracts with labor unions for future employment and payment of wages and benefits have not been considered as required disclosure items by the accounting profession. Instead, these are considered to be executory contracts, where the exact persons who will perform the work are not known. Also, there is a problem with the debit side of the entry. While it would be possible, for example, to compute the present value of the future costs likely under the newly-signed labor contract as a liability, what should be recorded as the offsetting debit?

There is some conceptual justification for considering adding this variable (pension and retirement costs) to the disclosure set of data presented in the financial statements. When the Financial Accounting Standards Board drafted its Conceptual Framework, one of the statements provided guidance for what information ought to be disclosed as accounting information which was useful (*Statement of Financial Accounting Concepts No. 2*, FASB 1980).

SFAC No. 2 provides that the two primary qualities of information which will enhance the data's usefulness for decision making purposes are relevance and reliability. Relevance is considered to be driven by predictive value, feedback value, and timeliness of information. Based on the results obtained in this research, it can be argued that there is now evidence that as union elections occur, changes will be found in pension and retirement costs of individual firms, compared to other members of the industry which do not have elections. Since it is desirable to have financial data which are comparable between firms and across time, disclosure of this item would enhance comparability of results between different firms. Timeliness refers to the receipt of the information by the user soon enough to have an effect on his or her decision making. Clearly not disclosing this data at all does little for the timeliness issue. It would remain for future testing to determine whether disclosure of the data annually would have an effect on users' decision making.

If the data are disclosed, and there has not been a completed transaction to be recorded, how should the data be disclosed? One suggestion for the disclosure format is to place the information in the text of the Notes to Financial Statements. Such notes are generally identified to specific account names in the statements by inserting a number after the account name, which refers the reader to the note of the same number. Some explanatory text would be useful to explain that the company had experienced labor union elections during the year just ended. This discussion could explain the name of the union, the net increase or decrease in union membership, and the effective date of the change. If this were a representation election, wherein the firm was being organized, it would be useful to disclose the length of the contract.

RESEARCH QUESTION 3

The third research question concerned profitability. Would return on investment be significantly different in firms with union elections compared to firms without union elections?

Return on investment has been tested earlier by Clark (1984). Clark found that ROI declined by 12 percent in firms which were unionized, and by adding controls for labor markets and market structure found that ROI for unionized firms was 19 percent below the sample mean.   This was based on 902 product-line businesses (segments, not complete firms) for the period 1970 to 1980.

The present research tested return on investment, using a later period of data, and found that there were no significant univariate differences, for either one year or two years after the election. Partitioning the datasets and examining differences by type of election and election outcome also failed to provide any significant explanatory power for election effects on ROI. When tested with an ANOVA, significant results were not obtained for the one year post-election data. Results for the two year post-election test were significant at the .05 alpha level for both election disposition and election type.

The results obtained in the present study contradicted those results obtained by Clark, and suggest various underlying issues. One possible explanation is the time lag from election to financial statement date. It is possible that at least two years' lag is necessary to capture these changes. This would be consistent with the results obtained for research question 1. A second issue, which is more basic to the measurement of these variables, is possible misspecification. However, given the prior research which has identified these variables as being influenced by labor activity, this does not seem appropriate. It appears, from the number of marginally significant results obtained in this study (e.g., significance at the .10 alpha level), that there is a linkage or an underlying force or event which causes these differences. That would suggest the variables used were less than perfect devices to capture the differences desired. This suggestion would help to explain why all the results obtained for pension and retirement expenditures were uniformly positive, even when that might not have seemed reasonable.

It was of interest to examine the different results obtained in the Clark study and the present one. Unlike the first two research questions, this research question focused on a variable which is less under the direct control of management or union and management. Return on investment is affected by many economic events in the life of the firm besides labor elections. Return on investment, defined as net income divided by total assets, is affected by investment or disposition of assets and by net income. The decision to invest in assets is influenced in part by tax policy such as the investment tax credit and depreciation rules. Net income is a result of performance itself, and as such is influenced by many other economic events besides a firm's labor elections, or lack thereof.

Clark's study had the advantage of a dataset which was based on business segments, while the present study used a single SIC code for each business. Since it is possible for any firm to have one group of employees unionized and another group nonunionized (i.e., at two different divisions) Clark's approach demonstrates that a very narrow definition of the business is required in order to differentiate union effects. This conclusion is further supported by the fact that Clark used a binary definition of unionism (either the product line business was unionized, or it was not). The present study likewise used a binary definition, but it was a measure of the existence of increase or decrease in the extent of unionism compared to similar firms which were stable in the level of their unionism (the control firms had no elections).

RESEARCH QUESTION 4

The last research question examined differences in productivity between firms with union elections and those without union elections. Productivity was defined as sales per employee. Performing t-tests of mean differences did not provide any significant results for either one year after the election or for two years after the election. When elections were tested by whether the union won or lost (for all election cases) in the one year post election the results were significant at alpha = .10. In this case, the test statistic was high and positive (1.937) with a p-value of 0.055, for elections which the union lost. This indicated a per-employee increase in sales of $1,937. This was compared with a negative test statistic (-1.060) for the reverse case, in which unions won the elections. This would suggest that per-employee sales was sensitive to the union "going away." In firms where unions lost a bid to enter (a representation election) or lost a bid to stay (a decertification election) the test statistic was significantly higher than in the control group firms with no elections. However, the ANOVA procedure for one year post-election did provide results which were significant at the .05 alpha level for per-employee sales. This was obtained on the election outcome variable. The ANOVA for two year post-election data did not provide any significant results.

This concludes the discussion of univariate findings. The multivariate analysis of variance was uniformly disappointing in the results obtained, but that was useful information in itself. The MANOVA testing of the four variables simultaneously (R&D, pensions, sales, and ROI) did not identify any significant results, in either the one year post-election data or the two year post-election data. This indicated that while there were a number of significant results found, none of these were enough to be identified when tested simultaneously. The results obtained suggest that there is a measurable phenomenon underlying the union effects, but that the phenomenon was not well captured in this research. If it had been, then the univariate results would have possibly been somewhat more significant and the phenomenon would have been identified in the multivariate testing.

Table V-1 presents a summary of the findings of this research. The significance attached to the findings varies.

The table also indicates that the time lag from election date to financial statement date may be important. This was the case for R&D and ROI for the two years post-election data. The strongest result for the pension variable was also found in the two year data for election disposition. In contrast, the results for the sales variable indicated that all significant influences were found within one year post-election. Other significant results were obtained for the pension variable in the one year data, but these were not as strong as that for the two year data.

Table V-1. Summary of findings.

Variables		P-value	Time Frame	Test
R&D	election held	.091	2 years	t-test
	election type	.073	2 years	ANOVA
Pensions	election held	.060	1 year	t-test
	disposition	.004	2 years	ANOVA
	representation	.094	1 year	t-test
ROI	election type	.023	2 years	ANOVA
	disposition	.039	2 years	ANOVA
Sales	disposition	.040	1 year	ANOVA
	decertification	.096	1 year	t-test
	disposition	.055	1 year	t-test

LIMITATIONS OF THIS STUDY

This study was constrained by using a single four-digit SIC code to classify each firm into an industry. This operated to reduce the number of observations which could be used, due to lack of suitable control firms. It was necessarily limited by requiring exact matches for accounting year-ends. This caused the loss of some observations which could not be matched to firms because of unusual months for the year-end. It was also limited by the quality and availabilty of the data on the Compustat tapes. Another limitation was that the labor election files from which the observations were drawn had to be edited to conform to firm names which could be matched to Compustat records. There was a limitation in that election data were available only in month and year of event format; the exact date of any form of union election was not available. It was assumed that the source data file was complete with respect to all election data. It was limited by a requirement in the design that observations used for testing must have had no other union elections for two years before or after the election year, effectively limiting the number of firms for testing to a smaller number than were available for event studies. This was thought necessary to eliminate confounding effects of other elections close to the period of the observation. Research and development data contained in Compustat were assumed to be correct. The reliability of this data was questioned for a test of 1972 data (San Miguel, 1977), the first year that such data were available through Compustat (Bublitz and Ettredge, 1989, 112, note 8). It was assumed that data for the period of this study were reliable.

AREAS FOR FUTURE RESEARCH

Based on the results of the tests for changes in pension and retirement costs, one specific area of future research would be a pilot test of additional disclosure of a sample of firms with union elections, to determine if there is any perceived increase in the utility of the data by analysts and investors. Based on the two year data for ROI, a longer-term test of this variable would also be of interest.

It would be interesting to seek other variables from Compustat which, when added to the variables in the current study, might produce significant results with multivariate tests. Examples are physical location of the plant site and the specific union involved.

Another aspect would involve testing the pre-election scores for the observations against the pre-election scores of the industry control groups, and likewise testing the post-election scores of the observations against the post-election scores of the controls. This would provide insight as to whether there were any differences in the pre- and post-event data. This would extend the present study, which was focused on a different primary question, which was whether there were differences over the time period surrounding an election.

SUMMARY AND IMPLICATIONS

This chapter has identified the key issues of this study of the financial effects of union elections on selected variables. As shown in Table V-1, significant results were obtained in a one year pre-election to one year-post election test, for sales per employee, and for pension and retirement benefits. The most significant results were found for the pension variable. Pension and retirement test statistics were uniformly positive and above the mean of control firms in all subgroups. This indicated that simply having an election was sufficient to influence this cost. Tests of data two years post-election provided significant results for ROI and R&D, and again for pensions. Suggestions were made regarding possible disclosure format in the financial statements. Prior research argued that pension data had been found to be desirable disclosure items, and its desirability was confirmed by empirical testing in the current study.

While each of the variables tested in this study generated findings which were significant at various levels, examining each of the research questions individually did not provide a clear answer to the main issue underlying this research. Each research question served as a proxy to help determine, in concert with the other questions, whether labor unions sufficiently affected firms that their relationship with the firm and its employees should become a required disclosure item. The research questions represented the areas in which prior studies had obtained significant results based on unionism. One of the contributions of this research was that it empirically tested these four areas of "union effects" in one study, using current data, in a longer-term test of union effects than is normally available.

Earlier it was argued that if significant results were obtained that would indicate differences between firms with labor elections and firms without labor elections. Table V-1 indicates that there was a union effect present in the current research. This effect was particularly evident in the pension variable, and in the R&D variable. For both of these measures of spending per employee, the fact that a labor election was held was found to be related to differences in pension costs and in R&D costs, both significant at the .10 alpha level. The results of the other two variables were not significant solely on the basis of whether elections were held. However, both return on investment and sales did provide significant results on two different subclassifications of elections each. For ROI, the type of election was related to differences between firms with elections and those without elections, which was significant at the .05 alpha level. Election outcome was also significantly related for ROI at the .05 alpha level.

Sales were significantly different for election outcome at the .05 alpha level and were also different for decertification elections, significant at the .10 alpha level.

Where does this lead us? This research attempted to test variables in each category for which prior studies reported significant results. Individually the tests provided results, for each variable tested, which were significant at different levels of alpha below .10.

This indicates there is a union effect, and there is a difference between firms with elections compared to those without elections. This in turn suggests there is an opportunity to improve the benefits of information disclosed through the annual financial statements. What are the benefits? To investors and analysts, the knowledge that firms with labor elections were "different" from firms without elections would allow such users to make more informed decisions with respect to equity investments. This would be useful information because it could be used to help explain interfirm differences. It could also prove useful at the industry level. Knowledge of particular union effects would prove beneficial when contemplating investment in an industry which one believed was about to become the object of union organizing efforts. As the best example in this study, pension costs for each subgroup studied were higher per employee than were those costs in the control firms without elections. This should be useful information to any investor or analyst, particularly as this cost is recurring.

The cost of this type of disclosure would be quite modest. It would require only footnote disclosure, and would not require substantive auditing of large volumes of transactions. The individual firm would be in the best position to access and provide the data, because it alone has access to the contract and has quicker access to the election data. The research results of this study provided affirmative answers to the research questions in all four variables tested. There was a union effect related to an election variable for research and development spending, pension and retirement costs, return on investment, and sales. Therefore the benefits to users of the financial statements should easily outweigh the modest costs of data collection. The disclosure of a firm's relationship with its union would provide demonstrated benefit to users at nominal cost to the firm.

SELECTED REFERENCES

Abdel-khalik, A. R. "The effect of LIFO-switching and firm ownership on executives' pay." *Journal of Accounting Research* Vol. 23, No. 2 (Autumn 1985): 427-447.

Afifi, A. A. and Virginia Clark. *Computer-Aided Multivariate Analysis* Second Edition. New York: Van Nostrand Reinhold, 1990.

Allen, S. G. "Productivity levels and productivity change under unionism." *Industrial Relations* Vol. 27, No. 1 (Winter 1988): 94-113.

Anderson, J. C., C. A. O'Reilly III, and G. Busman. "Union decertification in the U.S.: 1947-1977." *Industrial Relations* Vol. 19, No. 1 (Winter 1980). Research Notes: 100-107.

Bao, D. H., M. T. Lewis, W. T. Lin, and J. G. Manegold. "Applications of time-series analysis in accounting: a review." *Journal of Forecasting* Vol. 2, (1983): 405-423.

Bathke, A. W., Jr., K. S. Lorek, and G. L. Willinger. "Firm-size and the predictive ability of quarterly earnings data." *The Accounting Review* Vol. LXIV, No. 1, (January 1989): 49-68.

Becker, B. E. and C. A. Olson. "The impact of strikes on shareholder equity." *Industrial and Labor Relations Review* Vol. 39, No. 3 (April 1986): 425-438.

_____ and _____. "Unions and firm profits." *Industrial Relations* Vol. 31, No. 3 (Fall 1992): 395-415.

Belman, D. L. and P. B. Voos. "Wage effects of increased union coverage: methodological considerations and new evidence." *Industrial and Labor Relations Review* Vol. 46, No. 2 (January 1993): 368-380.

Bernstein, L. A. *Financial Statement Analysis: Theory, Application, and Interpretation* Fourth Edition. Homewood, Illinois: Richard D. Irwin, 1988.

Bigoness, W. J. and E. R. Peirce. "Responding to union decertification elections." *Personnel Administrator* Vol. 33 (August 1988): 49-53.

Bronars, S. G. and D. R. Deere. "Union representation elections and firm profitability." *Industrial Relations* Vol. 29, No. 1 (Winter 1990): 15-37.

Brown, C. and J. Medoff. "Trade unions in the production process." *Journal of Political Economy* Vol. 86, No. 3, (1978): 355-378.

Bublitz, B. and M. Ettredge. "The information in discretionary outlays: advertising, research, and development." *The Accounting Review* Vol. LXIV, No. 1, (January 1989): 108-124.

Buzby, S. L. "Selected items of information and their disclosure in annual reports." *The Accounting Review* (July 1974): 423-435.

Campbell, D. T. and J. C. Stanley. *Experimental and Quasi-Experimental Designs for Research.* Chicago: Rand McNally College Publishing Company, 1966.

Chandra, G. "A study of the consensus on disclosure among public accountants and security analysts." *The Accounting Review*, (October 1974): 733-742.

Clark, K. B. "The impact of unionization on productivity: a case study." *Industrial and Labor Relations Review* Vol. 33, No. 4, (July 1980): 451-469.

_____. "Unionization and firm performance: the impact on profits, growth, and productivity." *American Economic Review* Vol. 74, (December 1984): 893-919.

Cogger, K. O. "A time-series analytic approach to aggregation issues in accounting data." *Journal of Accounting Research* Vol. 19, No. 2, (Autumn 1981): 285-298.

Coleman, F. T. "Once a union, not always a union." *Personnel Journal* Vol. 64 (March 1985): 42-45.

Collins, W. A. and W. S. Hopwood. "A multivariate analysis of annual earnings forecasts generated from quarterly forecasts of financial analysts and univariate time-series models." *Journal of Accounting Research* Vol. 18, No. 2 (Autumn 1980): 390-406.

Connolly, R. A. and M. Hirschey. "R&D, market structure and profits: a value-based approach." *The Review of Economics and Statistics* Vol. LXVI, No. 4, (Nov. 1984): 682-686.

_____, B. T. Hirsch, and M. Hirschey. "Union rent seeking, intangible capital, and market value of the firm." *The Review of Economics and Statistics* Vol. 68 (November 1986): 567-577.

Dickens, W. T. and J. S. Leonard. "Accounting for the decline in union membership, 1950-1980." *Industrial and Labor Relations Review* Vol. 38, No. 3 (April 1985): 323-334.

Financial Accounting Standards Board. *Statements of Financial Accounting Concepts.* Homewood, Illinois: Richard D. Irwin, 1987.

Fossum, J. A. *Labor Relations: Development, Structure, Process.* Dallas: Business Publications, Inc., 1982.

Freeman, R. B. and J. L. Medoff. "New estimates of private sector unionism in the United States." *Industrial and Labor Relations Review* 32, (Jan. 1979): 143-174.

_____. "The effect of unionism on fringe benefits." *Industrial and Labor Relations Review* Vol. 34, No. 4 (July 1981): 489-509.

_____ and J. L. Medoff. "The impact of the percentage organized on union and nonunion wages." *The Review of Economics and Statistics* Vol. LXIII, No. 4, (Nov. 1981): 561-572.

_____ and _____. *What Do Unions Do?* New York: Basic Books, Inc. 1984.

Greer, C. R., S. A. Martin, and T. A. Reusser. "The effect of strikes on shareholder returns." *Journal of Labor Research* Vol. I, No. 2, (Fall 1980): 217-229.

Harrison, W. T., L. A. Tomassini, and J. R. Dietrich. "The use of control groups in capital market research." *Journal of Accounting Research* Vol. 21, No. 1 (Spring 1983): 65-77.

Herman, E. E., A. Kuhn, and R. L. Seeber. *Collective Bargaining and Labor Relations* (2nd edition) Englewood Cliffs, New Jersey: Prentice-Hall, Inc. 1987.

Hirsch, B. T. and A. N. Link. "Unions, productivity, and productivity growth." *Journal of Labor Research* Vol. V, No. 1, (Winter 1984): 29-37.

_____. "Firm investment behavior and collective bargaining strategy." *Industrial Relations* Vol. 31, No. 1 (Winter 1992): 95-121.

_____ and B. A. Morgan. "Shareholder risk and returns in union and nonunion firms." *Industrial and Labor Relations Review* Vol. 47, No. 2 (January 1994): 302-318.

Hirschey, M. and D. W. Wichern. "Accounting and market-value measures of profitability: consistency, determinants, and uses." *Journal of Business and Economic Statistics* Vol. 2, Number 4, (October 1984): 375-383.

Horwitz, B. and R. Kolodny. "The relationship between firm characteristics and the choice of financial measurement methods: an application to R&D." *Quarterly Review of Economics and Statistics* Vol. 21, No. 4, (Winter 1981): 75-86.

Huth, W. L. and D. N. MacDonald. "Equity market response to union decertification petitions and elections." *Journal of Labor Research* Vol. XI, No. 2 (Spring 1990): 193-201.

Imhoff, E. A. Jr. "Income smoothing: an analysis of critical issues."
Quarterly Review of Economics and Business Vol. 21, No. 3
(Autumn 1981): 23-42.

Karier, T. "Unions and monopoly profits." *The Review of Economics
and Statistics* Vol. 67, (February 1985): 34-42.

Kerlinger, F. N. *Foundations of Behavioral Research, Third Edition.*
New York: Holt, Rinehart and Winston, 1986.

Kilgour, J. G. "Decertifying a union: A matter of choice." *Personnel
Administrator* (July 1987): 42-51.

Kiss, R. M., L. J. Hexter, R. J. Curcio, and D. R. Williams. 1990.
The impact of labor strikes on shareholder wealth pre- and post-
PATCO. Paper presented at conference. Annual meeting of the
Financial Management Association.

Kokkelenberg, E. C. and D. R. Sockell. "Union membership in the
United States, 1973-1981." *Industrial and Labor Relations Review*
Vol. 38, No. 4, (July 1985): 497-543.

Lee, C. J. "Stochastic properties of cross-sectional financial data."
Journal of Accounting Research Vol. 23, No. 1 (Spring 1985):
213-227.

Link, A. N. "Basic research and productivity increase in
manufacturing: additional evidence." *American Economic Review*
Vol. 71, No. 5, (December 1981): 1111-1112.

_____. "Productivity growth, environmental regulations and the
composition of R&D." *Bell Journal of Economics* Vol. 13, No.
2 (Autumn 1982): 548-554.

Lustgarten, S. H. and S. B. Thomadakis. "Valuation response to new
information: a test of resource mobility and market structure."
Journal of Political Economy Vol. 88, No. 5, (Oct. 1980): 977-
993.

Manegold, J. G. "Time-series properties of earnings: a comparison of extrapolative and component models." *Journal of Accounting Research* Vol 19, No 2, (Autumn 1981): 360-373.

McFarland, H. "Evaluating q as an alternative to the rate of return in measuring profitability." *The Review of Economics and Statistics* Vol. LXX, No. 4 (Nov. 1988): 614-622.

Merkel, M. *The Labor Union Handbook.* New York: Beaufort Books, Inc., 1983.

Mitchell, M. W. and J. A. Stone. "Union effects on productivity: evidence from western U. S. sawmills." *Industrial and Labor Relations Review* Vol. 46, No. 1 (October 1992): 135-145.

Neely, W. P. and D. P. Rochester. "Operating performance and merger benefits: the savings and loan experience." *The Financial Review* Vol. 22, No. 1 (February 1987): 111-130.

Neumann, G. R. "The predictability of strikes: Evidence from the stock market." *Industrial and Labor Relations Review* Vol. 33, No. 4 (July 1980): 525-535.

Pakes, A. "On patents, R & D, and the stock market rate of return." *Journal of Political Economy* Vol. 93, No. 2, (April 1985): 390-409.

Pattillo, J. W. *The Concept of Materiality in Financial Reporting.* New York: The Research Foundation of Financial Executives Institute, 1976.

Pearce, T. G., J. E. Groff and J. R. Wingender. 1990. The impact of union decertification on shareholder wealth. Paper presented at conference. Annual meeting of the Financial Management Association.

Premeaux, S. R., R. W. Mondy, and A. Bethke. "Decertification: fulfilling unions' destiny?" *Personnel Journal* Vol. 66 (June 1987): 144-148.

Ravenscraft, D. J. "Structure-profit relationships at the line of business and industry level." *The Review of Economics and Statistics* Vol. 65 (1983): 22-31.

Ruback, R. S. and M. B. Zimmerman "Unionization and profitability: evidence from the capital market." *Journal of Political Economy* Vol. 92, Number 6, (December 1984): 1134-1157.

Salinger, M. A. "Tobin's q, unionization, and the concentration-profits relationship." *Rand Journal of Economics* Vol. 15, Number 2, (Summer 1984): 159-170.

San Miguel, J. G. "The reliability of R&D data in Compustat and 10-K reports." *The Accounting Review* Vol. LII, Number 3, (July 1977): 638-641.

Schwert, G. W. "Using financial data to measure effects of regulation." *The Journal of Law and Economics* Vol. XXIV (1) (April 1981): 121-158.

Shepherd, W. G. "The elements of market structure." *The Review of Economics and Statistics* Vol. 54, (Feb. 1972): 25-37.

Singhvi, S. S. and H. B. Desai. "An empirical analysis of the quality of corporate financial disclosure." *The Accounting Review*, (January 1971): 129-138.

Smirlock, M., T. Gilligan and W. Marshall. "Tobin's q and the structure-performance relationship." *American Economic Review* Vol. 74, Number 5, (December 1984): 1051-1060.

Standard & Poor's Compustat Services, Inc. 1990. *Industrial Compustat.* Englewood, Colorado: Standard & Poor's Compustat Services, Inc.

Thomadakis, S. B. "A value-based test of profitability and market structure." *The Review of Economics and Statistics* Vol. 59 (May 1977): 179-185.

Varela, O. "Using the COMPUSTAT tapes in studying the Dow Jones Portfolios." *Financial Analysts Journal* (September - October 1986): 70-75.

Voos, P. B. and L. R. Mishel. "The union impact on profits: evidence from industry price-cost margin data." *Journal of Labor Economics* Vol. 4, (January 1986): 105-133.

_____ and _____. "The union impact on profits in the supermarket industry." *The Review of Economics and Statistics* (August 1986): 513-517.

Weiss, L. W. "Average concentration ratios and industrial performance." *Journal of Industrial Economics* XII (1963): 37-54.

_____. "The concentration-profits relationship and antitrust" in *Industrial Concentration: The New Learning*, ed. Goldschmidt, H.J., H.M. Mann, and J.F. Weston, 185-223. Boston: Little, Brown and Company, 1974.

Wolk, H. I., J. R. Francis, and M. G. Tearney. *Accounting Theory: A Conceptual and Institutional Approach*. Boston: Kent Publishing Company, 1984.

APPENDICES

APPENDIX A.   Data Definitions.

Definitions of Compustat data items.   Quoted portions from the Compustat manual Data Definitions section.

SALES

Annual Compustat item 12. "This item represents gross sales (the amount of actual billings to customers for regular sales completed during the period) reduced by cash discounts, trade discounts, and returned sales and allowances for which credit is given to customers."

TOTAL ASSETS

Annual Compustat item 6. "Assets - total represents current assets plus net plant plus other noncurrent assets (including intangible assets, deferred items, and investments and advances)."

EMPLOYEES

Annual Compustat item 29.   "This item represents the number of company workers as reported to shareholders. This is reported by some firms as an average number of employees and by some as the number of employees at year-end. No attempt has been made to differentiate between these bases of reporting. If both are given, the year-end figure is used."

RESEARCH AND DEVELOPMENT EXPENSE

Annual Compustat item 46. "This item represents all costs incurred during the year that relate to the development of new products or services. This amount is only the company's contribution." Included are software expenses and amortization of software costs.

APPENDIX A.   Data Definitions.

NET INCOME

Annual Compustat item 172.   "This item represents the fiscal period income or loss reported by a company after subtracting expenses and losses from all revenues and gains." It includes the effects of discontinued operations, extraordinary items, income taxes, and minority interest.

PENSION AND RETIREMENT EXPENSE

Annual Compustat item 43.   "This item represents the pension and retirement expense included as an expense in the Income Statement. For defined benefit pension plans, this item represents either pension expense (pre-FASB #87) or net periodic pension cost (post-FASB #87).

APPENDIX B. Observations by Firm Name, SIC Code, and Election Date.

Firm Name	SIC Code	Election Year
Air Cargo Equipment Corp.	3443	1985
Alberto-Culver Co.	2844	1979
Allen Group	3714	1979
Aluminum Company of America	3334	1986
American Biltrite Inc.	3089	1979
American Healthcare Management	8062	1985
Arkla Inc.	4923	1979
Arrow Automotive Industries	3690	1980
Arvin Industries Inc.	3714	1979
Atlanta Gas Light Co.	4924	1987
Avon Products	2844	1982
AVX Corp.	3670	1983
Bankers Trust New York Corp	6022	1986
Base Ten Systems Inc.	3664	1985
Becton, Dickinson & Co.	3841	1983
Bio-Rad Laboratories	3826	1898
Borman's Inc.	5411	1984
Bristol-Myers Co.	2834	1979
Bristol-Myers Co.	2834	1986
Burlington Northern Inc.	4011	1985
Burndy Corp.	3678	1980
Cadbury Schweppes PLC	2000	1984
Calmat Co.	1400	1989
Carolina Power & Light	4911	1978
Castle & Cooke Inc.	0100	1980
Champion Parts Rebuilders	3714	1980
Charming Shoppes	5621	1980
Chicago Rivet & Machine Co.	3452	1984
Commonwealth Edison	4911	1988
Coleman Co.	3949	1981
Crane Co.	3490	1987
Dana Corp.	3714	1978
Dana Corp.	3714	1988

APPENDIX B. Observations by Firm Name, SIC Code, and Election
Date.   2 of 6

Firm Name	SIC Code	Election Year
Deltona Corp.	6552	1979
Dexter Corp.	2821	1988
Dillard Department Stores	5311	1980
Dow Jones & Co. Inc.	2711	1983
Duke Power Co.	4911	1981
Durakon Industries Inc.	3079	1989
Dynamics Corp. of America	3634	1980
E-Systems Inc.	3812	1981
Eaton Corp.	3714	1984
Eaton Corp.	3714	1986
EDO Corp.	3812	1979
EG&G Inc.	8711	1980
El Paso Electric Co.	4911	1987
Empire District Electric Co.	4911	1983
Energy Conversion Device	7391	1981
Engelhard Corp.	3330	1989
Essex Chemical Corp.	2810	1985
Facet Enterprises	3714	1983
Fairfield-Noble Corp.	2300	1982
Farmland Industries Inc.	2011	1987
Fays Drug Co.	5912	1980
Federal Signal Corp.	3711	1979
Ferro Corp.	2800	1986
Fischer & Porter Co.	3823	1980
Fischer & Porter Co.	3823	1983
Flame Industries Inc.	6799	1981
Gannett Co.	2711	1982
Gorman-Rupp Co.	3561	1989
Great Lakes Chemical Corp.	2800	1987
Green Mountain Power Corp.	4911	1986
Green Mountain Power Corp.	4911	1989
Greenman Brothers Inc.	5945	1981
Hamilton Digital Control Inc.	3689	1981

APPENDIX B. Observations by Firm Name, SIC Code, and Election
Date.

Firm Name	SIC Code	Election Year
Handy & Harman	3350	1980
Heekin Can Inc.	3411	1988
Helix Technology Corp.	3550	1979
Helmerich & Payne	1381	1988
Herley Microwave Systems Inc.	3679	1985
Hershey Foods Corp.	2060	1982
Hesston Corp.	3523	1980
Hexcel Corp.	3460	1978
Hickok Electrical Instruments	3925	1982
Houghton Mifflin Co.	2731	1978
Hydraulic Co.	4941	1979
ICN Pharmaceuticals Inc.	2834	1983
Illinois Power Co.	4931	1981
Illinois Power Co.	4931	1988
Insilco Corp.	3460	1979
Integrated Resources Inc.	6211	1984
Intel Corp.	3674	1978
Interco Inc.	2510	1978
Jacobson Stores	5311	1984
Kaiser Steel Corp.	1211	1979
Kansas Gas & Electric	4911	1979
Kansas Gas & Electric	4911	1985
Kansas Power & Light	4931	1986
Kasler Corp.	1600	1985
Koss Corp.	3651	1987
Krelitz Industries Inc.	5122	1979
Lawter International Inc.	2890	1985
Lee Pharmaceuticals	2844	1982
Lindberg Corp.	3390	1978
Liz Claiborne Inc.	2330	1988
Lone Star Industries	3241	1985
Longs Drug Stores Inc.	5912	1986
Lowe's Companies	5211	1979

APPENDIX B.   Observations by Firm Name, SIC Code, and Election
                      Date.   4 of 6

Firm Name	SIC Code	Election Year
Manitowoc Co.	3730	1981
Materials Research	3550	1978
May Department Stores Co.	5311	1985
Middlesex Water Co.	4940	1985
Minnesota Power & Light	4911	1980
Mobile Gas Service Corp.	4924	1978
Monarch Tile Manufacturing	3250	1979
Morton Thiokol Inc.	2890	1983
Morton Thiokol Inc.	2890	1986
Murphy Oil Corp.	2911	1982
Nalco Chemical Co.	2890	1980
National Education Corp.	8200	1987
National Healthcorp - LP	8051	1987
National Micronetics Inc.	3689	1986
National-Standard Co.	3310	1985
Nortek Inc.	3444	1979
Northeast Utilities	4911	1979
Northern Telecom Ltd.	3661	1986
Ohio Edison Co.	4911	1981
Ohio Edison Co.	4911	1984
Pico Products Inc.	3663	1986
Pitney-Bowes Inc.	3579	1977
Pitt-Desmoines Inc.	3443	1988
Plessey PLC	3812	1982
Ply-Gem Industries	2430	1986
Pope & Talbot Inc.	2621	1987
Pratt & Lambert Inc.	2851	1986
Public Service Co. of New Mexico	4931	1987
Publix Super Markets Inc.	5411	1987
Rauch Industries Inc.	3231	1984
Rochester Telephone Co.	4813	1982
Rockwell International Corp.	3721	1984
Rohm & Haas Co.	2821	1985

APPENDIX B. Observations by Firm Name, SIC Code, and Election
                      Date.   5 of 6

Firm Name	SIC Code	Election Year
Rohr Industries	3728	1977
Ryland Group Inc.	1531	1981
Savannah Electric & Power	4911	1988
Schering-Plough	2834	1978
Scott Paper Co.	2621	1988
Scott's Liquid Gold	2842	1981
Sealed Air Corp.	3089	1982
Sealed Air Corp.	3089	1989
Shaklee Corp.	2834	1982
Shawmut Corp.	6021	1980
Sherwin-Williams Co.	2851	1984
Sherwin-Williams Co.	2851	1986
Silvercrest Corp.	2451	1978
Simpson Industries	3714	1987
Smucker (J.M.) Co.	2033	1981
Southern California Water Co.	4940	1977
SPS Technologies Inc.	3452	1979
Square D Co.	3613	1984
Stanley Works	3420	1977
Standard Motor Products Inc.	3690	1981
Sterling Electronics	5065	1977
Stewart Sandwiches Inc.	2090	1986
Strawbridge & Clothier	5311	1980
Stride Rite Corp.	3140	1984
Superior Industries International	3714	1980
Superior Industries International	3714	1984
Sysco Corp.	5140	1989
Technical Coatings Inc.	2851	1987
Temple-Inland Inc.	2631	1989
Tenney Engineering Inc.	3569	1987
Teradyne Inc.	3825	1978
Texas Utilities Co.	4911	1983
Texas Utilities Co.	4911	1985

APPENDIX B. Observations by Firm Name, SIC Code, and Election
Date.   6 of 6

Firm Name	SIC Code	Election Year
Thermo Electron Corp.	1600	1983
Thomas & Betts Corp.	3640	1986
Thomas Industries Inc.	3640	1980
Timken Co.	3562	1984
Tootsie Roll Industries Inc.	2060	1981
Tower Properties Co.	6512	1988
Transitron Electronic Corp.	3678	1980
UGI Corp.	4932	1985
UMC Electronics Co.	3929	1986
United Brands	2011	1980
Utah Power & Light	4911	1981
United Telecommunications	4813	1978
Voplex Corp.	3714	1984
Washington Post Co.	2711	1989
Wells-Gardner Electronics	3690	1980
Westmoreland Coal Co.	1211	1982
Williams (W.W.) Co.	5080	1979
Woolworth (F.W.) Co.	5331	1984
Wyman-Gordon Co.	3460	1982
Zapata Corp.	1381	1984

APPENDIX C.   Observations Omitted from Analyses.
              One Year Post-Election Dataset

Purpose of Screening

    The observations which were used in testing were difference
scores. The calculation of this number was described in Chapter III in
the "Testing Design" section.
    This appendix reports observations which were removed from the
analysis and reported separately (Afifi and Clark, 1990, 37). The
distribution of data was examined for each of the various subgroups for
the magnitude of the values. Those deemed to be extreme relative to
the other values close to it were removed. Although they were the
actual values on the tape, they did not appear to represent "reasonable"
business results.
    Eight observations were discarded in the one year post-election
dataset. These eight are described below. Two observations were
discarded in the two years post-election dataset. This latter group is
presented after the one year outlier set. Observations are grouped
below for each of the four variables tested in the four hypotheses.

Company Name	Variable (Election Type)	Omitted Value	Next Closest Values
Energy Conversion Device	R&D/employee	-$ 23,289	-$ 2,631
			-$ 1,062
			-$ 685
Northern Telecom	R&D/employee	$ 17,402	$ 933
			$ 922
			$ 591

    Two observations were removed from this dataset for per-
employee research and development expenditures.

Company Name	Variable (Election Type)	Omitted Value	Next Closest Values
Tower Properties	Sales/employee	$324,813	$231,813* $ 95,228 $ 78,994
El Paso Electric	Sales/employee	$231,813	$ 95,228 $ 78,994 $ 72,457
Integrated Resources	Sales/employee	-$169,542	-$ 80,523 -$ 76,579 -$ 69,623

Three observations were removed from the one year post-election dataset for the per-employee sales variable.

Company Name	Variable (Election Type)	Omitted Value	Next Closest Values
Becton Dickinson	ROI	-2.9635	-1.4568* -0.3107 -0.3104
Lee Pharmaceuticals	ROI	-1.4568	-0.3107 -0.3104 -0.2768
UMC Electronics	ROI	1.6954	0.9834 0.7160 0.5977

Three observations were deleted from the one year post-election dataset for return on investment.

Legend: * = observation also removed as an outlier.

APPENDIX C. Observations Omitted from Analyses.
             Two Year Post-Election Dataset

Company Name	Variable (Election Type)	Omitted Value	Next Closest Values
Energy Conversion Device	R&D/employee	$ 18,275	$ 1,632
			$ 810
			$ 367

One observation was removed from the two years post-election dataset for the per-employee research and development expenditures variable.

Company Name	Variable (Election Type)	Omitted Value	Next Closest Values
Becton Dickinson	ROI	-2.9370	-1.0608
			-0.4571
			-0.2920

One observation was removed from the two years post-election dataset for the return on investment variable.

APPENDIX D. T-test of Mean Differences for Size Between Observations and Control Groups, by Number of Employees and Total Assets.

A univariate t-test of mean differences was performed to determine if there were significant differences between the observations and control groups for two measures of size, number of employees and total assets. This was included in the test procedures to provide assurance that there were no material differences in the variables used for testing the hypotheses which might be attributed to firm size. A finding of significant results would lead to possibly different interpretations of the data analyzed. The results of the test appear below.

	Number of Employees	Total Assets
Sample size:	178	179
Ho: Mean $\neq$ 0		
Statistic	-0.910	0.542
P-value	0.364	0.588

INDEX

157